The Kingdom Perspective

The Kingdom Perspective

Reflections from an Ordinary Person Living an
Extraordinary Life All Because of Jesus

LIZA KOBAYASHI

authorHOUSE®

AuthorHouse™
1663 Liberty Drive
Bloomington, IN 47403
www.authorhouse.com
Phone: 1-800-839-8640

Published by AuthorHouse   12/06/2012

ISBN: 978-1-4772-8817-7 (sc)
ISBN: 978-1-4772-8815-3 (hc)
ISBN: 978-1-4772-8816-0 (e)

Library of Congress Control Number: 2012921324

Contents

Dedication

*To all Jesus seekers who desire to see His
Kingdom fully established on Earth
As it already is in Heaven

*To My Beloved Family

*To Jesus

Acknowledgements

*to the love of my life-
Dwight—my soul mate, "my man" & best friend
You have always believed the best in me & supported
me in all that the Lord has asked. You love me like
Jesus does. I am deeply blessed. I love you!

*to my 3 greatest treasures on Earth-
Kyla, Kairos & Kailee
Thank you for allowing mom to be a part of your
faith journey on Earth. Jesus teaches me so much
through each of you. I ♥ you and am glad
we're family forever.

*to Koby, my firstborn son in Heaven-
It is through you that this journey of the reality
of God's Kingdom all began. I love you son. I look
forward to the day I will see you face to face.

*to Carolyn Suty-
spiritual mom, friend & fellow artist
Thanks again for your love, encouragement and
prayers. I will never forget your gentle "push" to
write and to become an author in obedience to God.

*to Mama Sue Erickson-
spiritual mentor/mom
Thank you for those many years that you poured
your time, wisdom, discernment, prayers & love
into my life. I am so grateful for you & Papa
Erickson.*

*to Daniel Kikawa, Vernie R., Carolyn, Sue,
my sister Lisa Nagamine & Jenna Alipaz-
Thank you for going through the manuscript & for
sharing your counsel, discernment, feedback &
editing skills with me. I am grateful.*

*to Leila Fujinaka & my fellow intercessors-
Thank you for your love, encouragement, prayers
and intercession. I am blessed!*

foreword

A Word from my Spiritual Moms:

Carolyn Suty
U.S. Regional Director
Aglow International

Liza has an endearing way of inviting you into her world, sharing her daily walk & life with Jesus, and her love with precious husband Dwight and their four children, Koby, Kyla, Kairos and Kailee. You will learn powerful truths as you read her experiences and the things she gleamed in her listening times with God. I found myself marveling at the supernatural way this family moves together as a unit as I read their journey & how their marriage, family and lifestyle are central to the Kingdom Perspective.

In this book, Liza begins to reveal powerful insights on the requirements of the Kingdom and I am embracing the visions and dreams presented. She also shares about the keys to the kingdom which leads to the righteous life in Him: the pitfalls of not seeking Him first in all things, our vital need for humility and the crucial importance of our willingness to be led by Him each step of the way in our lives.

This book is a timely message and also a warning to the body of Christ. He is coming soon. Are we prepared spiritually & mentally for the days ahead? Liza talks about preparing ourselves spiritually by having our eyes cemented on Him, our ears hearing His voice and His words of faith, and the call for each one of us not to judge but to see the plan of God. Unity is key to the Kingdom.

This book challenged me in a profound way. Liza and Dwight's first son is with Jesus. They yielded their son to God for His plans and purposes. Their hearts' cry when he died was, "Whatever brings You greater glory." As Jesus' return draws near, this family knows it will cost them everything. This is the cost of serving Him. Are we willing to walk in this place for Him? Are we yielded vessels that will surrender all if He asks? The Kingdom Perspective is a must read to understand the challenge of the times we are living in today.

Are you ready? Do you know Him as King, Friend, & Savior? You will want to know Him more and more as you read this book.

———

Susan Erickson

Former Director of Discipleship of Nth Heights Lutheran Church, St. Paul, Mn.
Coordinator and Pastor of Uplink Groups
for Arise! Women's Ministry, St. Paul, Mn.

"Thy kingdom come, Thy will be done on earth as it is in Heaven" is a prayer that has been prayed intensely by the body of Christ. I believe God is answering this prayer by directing Liza to put into writing what He has been teaching her and what she has journaled as to what this will look like in each believer's life. As you journey with her through her many encounters with the Holy Spirit, you will discover the power of intimacy. You will come to know the love of God, experience a supernatural increase in childlike faith, radically increase your expectation of His desire to be present in your life, and be challenged to a higher call and commitment.

The Holy Spirit is eager to come in many ways to the children. As Liza says in her book, "There is no junior Holy Spirit!" As my husband and I read and reread this family's experiences of intimacy, we were given a greater vision of how God wants to come to the children and speak through them. You will understand how He wants all ages prepared for what lies ahead. Each chapter is full of treasures to be explored and truths to be taken hold of. I highly recommend this book as you seek first His Kingdom.

———

A Word from my Husband Dwight:

Behavioral Health Specialist/Counselor/
Social Worker at Hilo High School
Pastor of Elevate Church in Hilo, Hawaii

Liza and I have witnessed the reality and power of Jesus moving in our household. It's nothing I have ever seen or experienced before. And I know a lot of it has to do with Liza, starting in the secret place. That's where most of this book comes from—Liza & Jesus spending quality time together.

Although I am admittedly quite biased in saying the following, please know that it is absolutely true . . . Liza has the most "real" relationship with Jesus of anyone I know! His presence, and the fruit that comes while walking in Him, are so evident in her life. It's almost tangible. Just ask my kids (because you can't fool kids with stuff like this!) . . . Jesus is very real in Liza. Because of this, He is all the more real in our household. He has become more than just mommy and daddy's Jesus. He is now <u>their</u> Jesus. They know Him. Why? Because His Kingdom is real, not just up in heaven, but between our carpet and the ceiling!

Of course we have just as many "bad hair days" as anyone else, but when the perfection (Jesus) inhabits a household, it's a lot easier to focus on Him than the clay pots (us). I think that's a lot of what you will get in these pages . . . snap-shots of Jesus working in and through Liza (and our family). Hopefully you will become captivated by the eternal Creator as He does His thing amongst His kids. That's the kingdom perspective . . . our real Jesus, right here, right now . . . in us.

Prologue

Vision
3/2/08
Journal Entry:

During a time of waiting silently before the Lord, I saw myself with Jesus. He was dressed in white and He was holding my hand. He took me to the same cliff He had shown me before.

The first time He had shown me this place, there was a huge valley below. It was filled with different army camps. Each of the armies had beautiful tents and banners. From looking at the various styles, designs and colors of these tents and banners, however, it was clear that these army camps were individualistic and not unified. The camps were all separated and scattered through out the valley. At that particular time, the Lord had told me that this represented the state of His army (the Church).

This second time, as I stood with Him on the cliff and looked down in the valley, no longer did I see individual camps. Instead there was one huge army and all the groups were unified. There was a red theme throughout the military encampment. There were still tents in different styles (and I sensed it may have to do with different nations and movements). I saw banners blowing in the wind over different groups that were as beautifully ornate and exquisite as the tents. Over the entire army, however, I saw one huge banner flying overhead. On it was written in bold capital letters, "MY KINGDOM." Then I saw some of the people in His army close up as they came out of the tents. Although they were clothed in different cultural & ethnic styles, they were all dressed as royalty and in white. They were beautiful and glorious to behold.

Chapter 1
The Beginning . . .

On April 18th, 1997, my life and the life of my husband were changed forever with the birth of our firstborn child Koby. He lived for just 4-5 hours. Death is deeply painful to encounter, especially when it takes the life of someone very close and dear to your heart. When Koby passed away, I had to wrestle not just with death, but with the truth of the finality and shortness of life, with the truth that our lives on Earth are but a vapor in time and surprisingly, with the truth of heaven. Honestly, before my son died, I lived with heaven being some kind of happy thought that I tucked at the back of my mind that I knew would come at the end of my life. But as the Lord walked me and my husband Dwight through this road of suffering and loss, He began to show us something that filled our hearts to overflow with hope—the reality and truth of Jesus' heavenly kingdom.

We were changed forever by his short life. Within a year of his passing, I began to sense the Lord asking me to write about what we walked through with the loss of our son. To be honest, it seemed an impossible task both for my heart and for my lifestyle, which in that season included teaching high school science full time. After my second child was born, I quit teaching to become a full time mom. But I still didn't have the courage or passion to write. Year after year, the call from the Lord to write Koby's story increased in intensity until finally, after receiving prophetic words about being an author from deeply respected and proven leaders over a span of 7 years, getting confirmations from those in spiritual authority over me, and having the full blessing, support and agreement from my wonderful husband, I finally obeyed the Lord and wrote <u>Whatever Brings You Greater Glory</u> published in December of 2004.

Immediately after the book was completed and printed, I felt both ecstatic and relieved. Ecstatic in that I finally wrote and published the book, which I knew was a huge miracle and divine act of God; relieved in that I would never have to do that again. At least, that's what I thought. I remember letting out a deep sigh of relief and telling myself, "Whew! Glad that's over! I obeyed God and now my short term 'career' as an author is done! I won't have to do that ever again."

One week later, I was spending time being still before the Lord, waiting on Him in silence when I heard him "speak" to my heart. "By the way Liza . . ." My heart started thumping as I thought, "Oh no." I then responded in my heart, "Yes Lord?" "Liza, I want you to write a second book and I want you to entitle it <u>The Kingdom Perspective</u>." My heart stopped as my mind screamed, "WHAT? You're kidding right? You want me to write another book? And what the heck is "The Kingdom Perspective" anyway? How can I write a book on something I am clueless about? This is intimidating Lord. Who am I to write a book on that subject? I thought I was done writing!"

Yes, I was complaining. Sorry. Just being blunt honest. Eventually, I finally stopped and repented to the Lord for my bickering and complaining. And as I asked the Lord to confirm what He told me, He immediately gave me the following verse: *Jeremiah 30:2 (NAS)—"Thus says the LORD, the God of Israel, Write all the words which I have spoken to you in a book."*

So I simply surrendered. "Ok Jesus. I love You. If this is what You want me to do, I will do it. Whatever brings You greater glory Lord. If You want me to write this book, I'll write it. But You have to help me. Be it done to me according to Your will."

Right after this, I heard absolutely nothing about it from Jesus for over 1 year. (Doesn't our God have His own unique sense of humor?) During this season of silence, I would find myself doubting the Lord's call to write this 2nd book. The following questions would batter my mind. "Lord, did I miss the boat?" "Were my spiritual ears tone deaf that day and I just heard my own flesh or the enemy?" I would catch myself worrying and stressing out about what and how to write this 2nd book. And I would find myself once more in a fierce battle with my mind. "Who am I to 'teach' on this subject Lord?" "Jesus, I'm just a stay home mom. I'm not a theologian!" "How the heck am I going to even start this task?"

Now, you've got to realize that this was at the end of 2004; and throughout 2005, the "kingdom of heaven" wasn't yet a buzz phrase that a lot of people were talking about—at least not in my world. Since then, the kingdom of heaven is something most followers of Jesus are talking about, which is a God thing.

Going back to *Jeremiah 30:2 (NAS)*—*"Thus says the LORD, the God of Israel, Write all the words which I have spoken to you in a book."* I found this verse personally very confirming. Because of it, I've tried to vigilantly write those things He had spoken and shown me down in my journals. That is why most of this book contains journal entries of these special times with Jesus.

I have to confess, I still stressed out between doubt, unbelief and self-pity about writing this manuscript. The Lord did later speak to my heart about it. "Liza, when I asked you to write this book, <u>The Kingdom Perspective</u>, I wasn't asking you to write it like a theologian or expert. All I want you to do is to write about My Kingdom through your eyes. It will be a living testimony of how I can move through a family—a housewife & homemaker, 3 kids, and a godly man/husband." Immediately I felt a tremendous sense of relief and peace. Thank you Jesus!

As I journeyed with Jesus in completing this manuscript, I honestly found the task of writing on this topic "The Kingdom Perspective" quite daunting and overwhelming. Questions would plague my mind. "Who am I to write a book on this subject?" "What if people get offended?" "Lord, are you sure you want me to share that in the book?" But as my eyes refocused on Jesus, and I would spend time with Him in the secret place, I would be deeply encouraged by the things He would speak and show me about this manuscript and the things He desired to do through it.

I have one more confession to make. As I finished this manuscript, I wrestled with publishing this book with the title, "**The** Kingdom Perspective." "Lord, can I change it? You know, why not entitle it, "**A** Kingdom Perspective." I bet a lot more people will be less offended if I use the word "A" versus "The." Perhaps this may make picking up the book and reading it more palatable. Also Jesus, some people may think I am prideful, having a title with the word "The" implying that what I share in this book is the only perspective or the main perspective. They may think I am full of myself & pride and that I'm trying to push my own agenda."

As I wrestled with the Lord, I was quickly reminded by the Holy Spirit of my personal struggle with the fear of man and wanting to be accepted and approved by people. He also reminded me that this was the title He gave me way back in December of 2004 when He first told me about writing a 2nd book. Simply put, this was the title that He wanted for it.

So after repenting to Jesus for fearing man and desiring the approval of man over Him, I have chosen to be obedient to Him. I am deeply sorry if the title offended any of you. But I need to be faithful and obedient to Jesus above all else. So the title of this book is The Kingdom Perspective.

Looking back over these 8+ years since He gave me this assignment, I am relieved that I finally finished it—through His help, power and leading. The main reason why I wrote this book was simply because Jesus asked me to. Because I deeply love him, I want to obey Him. So I did it. The things I have shared in this manuscript come from my own experiences with Him and from the things He has shown & taught me; mainly while I have been with Him in the secret place of intimacy, waiting on Him in silence and listening to His voice.

It is my prayer that as you read this book, the Holy Spirit would reveal His truth and His heart through it. As always, please take only what you sense is of Him. Every follower of Jesus has been given a piece of revelation, a piece of the tapestry, not the whole picture. And no one is perfect. What I share in this book is simply my piece. *Revelations 12:11 (NAS) states:* **"And they overcame him because of the blood of the Lamb and because of the word of their testimony, and they did not love their life even when faced with death."** It is my hope that this book would bring our King Jesus greater glory on Earth, and that God would use it to help you have an even clearer perspective of His Kingdom, so that you would be better equipped as a soldier in His last days army to overcome the evil one.

So in obedience, I share this book with you-my testimony of Jesus and His Kingdom through the things He's shown me in the secret place. It is a simple collection of reflections from an ordinary person living an extraordinary life all because of Jesus.

Chapter 2
His Kingdom

As a child, I was always fascinated with fairy tales about kingdoms, princesses & knights. I loved the vivid descriptions of the castles, battles and the royal court. And my favorite part was the ending. Evil looked like it was going to triumph over good, when suddenly the hero rode in to the scene on a white horse. You could see passion pulsating through his body as love overflowed out of his heart through his eyes for His beloved. He was always clothed in white, positioned at the front of his army, while He charged fearlessly into battle. His army was usually outnumbered but that didn't matter. Wielding a huge sword, He led His troops forward as he fearlessly pulverized the enemy with His powerful sword. Swiftly and deftly, the enemy forces were whittled down and then the battle was over. He always won! Then the hero rode to the side of his beloved. With deep passion, desire and love flowing from his heart, he would sweep her off her feet and carry her onto his horse. Then the two would ride off into the sunset forever. The End.

Growing up, I would see these themes being played out over and over again in movies and books. Good defeats evil. Love conquers all. Justice prevails. The righteous kingdom wins and rules over the unrighteous one. And even now, I've found that these things still hit a deep place in my heart. So what is it about these themes that seem to transcend time, age and even gender and culture?

For me, perhaps these things hit my heart so deeply because they are like a fleeting shadow at best of the most beautiful kingdom and noble hero that really does exist.

Psalm 103:19 (NIV)—
"The LORD has established his throne in heaven, and his kingdom rules over all."

According to Strong's Concordance, the Hebrew word for kingdom in this verse is "malkuwth" (mal-kooth') and it's defined as royalty, royal power, reign, kingdom, sovereign power, dominion, realm. The word "all" comes from the Hebrew word "kol" (kole), which is defined as all, the whole of, any, each, every, anything, totality, everything. Finally, the word for heaven in this verse comes from the Hebrew word "shamanism" (shaw-mah'-yim) and is defined as heaven, heavens, sky (visible heavens, sky as abode of the stars, as the visible universe), atmosphere, and heaven as the abode of God.

Therefore, Psalm 103:19 declares that the LORD has established His throne in heaven and that His kingdom rules over all which includes the Earth and all of its inhabitants. Now when Jesus, the Son of God, came to Earth, His mind was focused on His Father and His Father's kingdom. How do we know that? In Matthew 4:17 (ESV), as Jesus began His ministry, He preached and proclaimed a simple message—*"Repent, for the kingdom of Heaven is at hand." Matthew 4:23 (ESV) states "And He went throughout all of Galilee . . . proclaiming the gospel of the kingdom."* In John 18: 36-37 (NIV), when questioned by Pontius Pilate before He was crucified, Jesus talked about His kingdom. He said, *"My kingdom is not of this world. If it were, my servants would fight to prevent my arrest by the Jews. But now My kingdom is from another place." "You are a king, then!" said Pilate. Jesus answered, "You are right in saying I am a king. In fact, for this reason I was born, and for this I came into the world, to testify to the truth. Everyone on the side of truth listens to me."*

In these passages, Jesus clearly described Himself as the King of a kingdom that was not of this world. He defined this kingdom as being found in another dimension (the heavenly realm). In the bible, this kingdom is also described as having a real throne room. In Revelation 4 (ESV), the beloved disciple John gave an account of what he saw in a vision.

"After this I looked, and behold, a door standing open in heaven! And the first voice, which I had heard speaking to me like a trumpet, said, "Come up here, and I will show you what must take place after this." At once I was in the Spirit, and behold, a throne stood in heaven, with one seated on the throne. And he who sat there had the appearance of jasper and carnelian, and around the throne was a rainbow that had the appearance of an emerald. Around the throne were twenty-four thrones, and seated on the thrones were twenty-four elders, clothed in white garments, with golden crowns on their heads. From the throne came flashes of lightning, and rumblings and peals of thunder, and before the throne were burning seven torches of fire, which are the seven spirits of God, and before the throne there was as it were a sea of glass, like crystal. And around the throne, on each side of the throne, are four living creatures, full of eyes in front and behind: the first living creature like a lion, the second living creature like an ox, the third living creature with the face of a man, and the fourth living creature like an eagle in flight. And the four living creatures, each of them with six wings, are full of eyes all around and within, and day

and night they never cease to say "Holy, Holy, Holy, is the Lord God Almighty, who was and is and is to come!" And whenever the living creatures give glory and honor and thanks to him who is seated on the throne, who lives forever and ever, the twenty-four elders fall down before him who is seated on the throne and worship him who lives forever and ever. They cast their crowns before the throne, saying, "Worthy are you, our Lord and God to receive glory and honor and power for you created all things and by your will they existed and were created."

Isn't this awesome? And it's real! Now what about that noble hero? In Revelations 19:11-16 (ESV), the bible describes Jesus.

"Then I saw heaven opened, and behold, a white horse! The one sitting on it is called Faithful and True, and in righteousness he judges and makes war. His eyes are like a flame of fire, and on his head are many diadems, and he has a name written that no one knows but himself. He is clothed in a robe dipped in blood, and the name by which he is called is The Word of God. And the armies of heaven, arrayed in fine linen, white and pure, were following him on white horses. From his mouth comes a sharp sword with which to strike down the nations, and he will rule them with a rod of iron. He will tread the winepress of the fury of the wrath of God the Almighty. On his robe and on his thigh he has a name written, King of kings and Lord of lords."

The King of Kings and Lords of Lords, Jesus, is really going to return to Earth riding on a magnificent white horse and He is coming to judge the Earth and save His bride, the church. And His bride will, in a sense, be swept off her feet to be with Him forever.

So why did I just share these things with you? Before Koby died, I knew all these facts and truth in my head. I've factually known that Jesus was King of His kingdom in heaven since I was a child. But to be blatantly honest, these truths of God's Kingdom were part of my "happy file" of eternity that I kept at the back of my brain that I would only pull out when I attended funerals or when I thought about getting old and dying.

But when Dwight and I faced death head-on when our son died, we were brought face to face with the truths of who Jesus really is and of His heavenly kingdom. Since 1997, Dwight and I have gratefully become desperate for more of Jesus. We now know in our hearts and not just in our heads that **this kingdom is real and that Jesus is the only thing worth seeking in this lifetime.**

In my desperation and hunger for more of Him, I've spent countless hours daily waiting before the Lord, many times in silence especially over the past 8+ years. And by His grace and only by His blood, I have found Jesus so faithful in meeting me in this place of deep intimacy.

William Barclay once said, **"Prayer is not a way of making use of God; prayer is a way of offering ourselves to God in order that He should be able to make use of us. It may be that one of our great faults in prayer is that we talk too much and listen too little. When prayer is at its highest, we wait in silence for God's voice to us."**

What I have personally found is that prayer's primary focus needs to be rooted in intimacy with Him; encountering God, listening to His heart/voice, then praying, interceding, & declaring what He tells and shows us. It is not simply rattling off my list of needs. God isn't looking for a particular method or perfection. Whew! But I know He's looking for faith and for friendship.

Psalm 25:13-15 (ESV)
"His soul shall abide in well-being, and his offspring shall inherit the land.
The friendship of the LORD is for those who fear him,
and he makes known to them his covenant.
My eyes are ever toward the LORD, for he will pluck my feet out of the net."

It has been a joy and a privilege to grow in my personal friendship with Jesus, especially since our son Koby died. These past 15 years since our son's passing have been filled with lessons of learning to wait in silence before Him, of experiencing His sweet presence, of learning to discern His voice and of listening to Him share the things on His heart from His perspective. It is from this place of intimate friendship with Jesus that He's chosen to show me many of the things about His kingdom and about Himself that I share in this book. Most are through journal entries that address Jesus in the first person.

Chapter 3
A Matter of Perspective

It's funny how 2 people can be in the same room, walk through the same situation and then see things from 2 totally different perspectives. When Dwight and I were engaged, we had an experience that demonstrated this. We were driving in his blue Toyota Camry up a steep incline on the freeway. As we came over the top of the hill, we both simultaneously gasped. I gasped in frustration as my eyes were stunned by the bumper-to-bumper traffic that lay before us and my brain began to do the math, calculating how long it would take for us to go through this traffic until we reached our destination. Dwight's gasp was one of sheer awe and delight as his eyes focused on the beautiful orange sky and stunning sunset that filled the heavens over the traffic. We both saw the same scene. Yet our reactions were so different. **It's amazing how what we allow ourselves to focus on and with what type of perspective we're viewing it determines how much of life we truly live.**

"Whether we see accurately is not determined by what we are looking at, but rather from the perspective with which we are viewing it. Are we looking from God's perspective or man's?"
Rick Joyner

This is godly wisdom. It is wise to always inquire of the Lord and to ask Him to show us how He sees things so that we will have His perspective and not man's or our own fleshly ones.

When I looked up the word "perspective" online, I found the following definitions: "the art of drawing three-dimensional solid objects on a two-dimensional surface so as to give the right impression of their height, width, depth, and position in relation to each other when viewed from a particular point; a view or prospect; a particular way of regarding something; understanding of the relative importance of things."

When I use the phrase, "Kingdom Perspective" in this book, I am defining it as "a particular way of regarding something/a view based upon the belief of the supremacy and reality of the spiritual reign and authority of God." It is the understanding of the relative importance of things through this view of the Kingdom and Supremacy of God and the belief that we truly are citizens of heaven and are just foreigners on Earth. (Phil. 3:19-21) In a "nutshell", I am simply defining "Kingdom Perspective" as **seeing things as God sees them**.

In the following sections, I will share some kingdom perspectives that He has shared with me while I've spent time with Him. I know I only see in part and again the things I share in this book are simply the pieces He's given to me. I pray the Lord would release a supernatural increase of His Spirit of Wisdom and Revelation in you as you read these chapters and that you would be granted deeper revelation, illumination and understanding into the things of His Kingdom.

Chapter 4
Kingdom Perspective on Marriage
Let marriage be held in honor among all.

2/6/09
Journal entry:

Early in the morning, about 5 am, I woke up and was waiting on the Lord when I got the following picture. I saw a place of bricks, tiles and an unfinished project. Then I fell asleep. Finally, at about 11:30 am, as I was really awake and waiting on the Lord, the Holy Spirit reminded me that I needed to get the rest of the picture (that there was something important He still needed to show me). As I refocused, I got the following picture.

I saw a woman with a white hat on hunched to the ground. She was clothed in white. I sensed she was really old even though I couldn't see her face and I didn't know who she was. On the ground was a huge unfinished project. It looked like an unfinished pathway. Then Jesus spoke. "This represents the DNA of Elevate (my home church). It's still being built." Then He extended an open hand to me. In the center of his palm was a small tile with the word "marriage" written on it. Then He spoke again. "I want marriage to be held in honor by all & to be a part of the DNA of Elevate. Open your hands." So I did. Then He dropped the tile gently into my hands. As I held it, I could feel how powerful and precious marriage was to Him. Then He said, "Hand this tile to that woman."

"Okay." I responded. Then I gave the tile to her. As I did, I immediately knew who she was. "Jesus, she is wisdom, isn't she." He responded "Yes." Suddenly, she had her hands filled with many tiles, all with "marriage" written on them. Then she began to walk all over the unfinished project, bending over and adding/gluing in these tiles that represented "marriage being held in honor" into it.

———

In Hebrews 13:1-8 (ESV), Paul listed sacrifices
that please God.

*"Let brotherly love continue. Do not neglect to show hospitality to strangers, for thereby some have entertained angels unawares. Remember those who are in prison, as though in prison with them, and those who are mistreated, since you also are in the body. **Let marriage be held in honor among all**, and let the marriage bed be undefiled, for God will judge the sexually immoral and adulterous. Keep your life free from the love of money, and be content with what you have, for he has said, "I will never leave you nor forsake you." So we can confidently say, "The Lord is my helper; I will not fear; what can man do to me?" Remember your leaders, those who spoke to you the word of God. Consider the outcome of their way of life, and imitate their faith. Jesus Christ is the same yesterday and today and forever."*

In these verses, we are admonished to love our brothers & sisters in Christ, to love strangers, to love prisoners, to help those mistreated, to honor marriage, to not love money, to be content, and then to ultimately trust God. Isn't it something that in the midst of this list, smack dab in the middle, is the command, "Honor marriage"?

Today, I know many young adults in the Christian world that are sick of religion & want the church to be relevant to a lost & dying world. (Me too.) They are not into being Sunday pew dwellers that just want to be spoon-fed spiritual tidbits once a week & who then live life as they want for the next 6 days. They desire being real and transparent versus wearing masks and pretending everything is okay. They don't buy into the American Dream. Instead, this generation of followers of Jesus desire true social justice. They want to be the hands & feet of Jesus. This is awesome!

Just as much as it's important to grow in love and community, to do social justice by reaching out beyond our church walls to the mistreated and less fortunate in our city, to not love money, to be content with what you have and to trust God, it is also vital and we are commanded to honor marriage. "Let marriage be held in honor among all, and let the marriage bed be undefiled, for God will judge the sexually immoral and adulterous."

We can't be into social justice but then be totally lax about sexual immorality, fornication and adultery. If we are going to be all about filling the world with the worship of Jesus, then we need to be a church & movement where marriage is held in honor among all and where we will not defile the marriage bed with fornication or adultery.

There are 3 things listed in scripture that overcome and conquer the evil one. It's the blood of Jesus, the word of our testimony and our willingness to die for Christ.

Revelation 12:11 (ESV)
And they have conquered him by the blood of the Lamb
and by the word of their testimony, for they loved not their
lives even unto death.

We can be missional, make great sacrifices, & give up all that we have to feed the poor. But if in the midst of this pursuit, Dwight and I suddenly announced to everyone that we were getting a divorce, it would instantly destroy the word of our testimony, or at the very least, greatly weaken it.

Jesus loves marriage. He created this beautiful relationship.

Ephesians 5:22-33 (The Message) says, "Wives, understand and support your husbands in ways that show your support for Christ. The husband provides leadership to his wife the way Christ does to his church, not by domineering but by cherishing. So just as the church submits to Christ as he exercises such leadership, wives should likewise submit to their husbands. Husbands, go all out in your love for your wives, exactly as Christ did for the church—a love marked by giving, not getting. Christ's love makes the church whole. His words evoke her beauty. Everything he does and says is designed to bring the best out of her, dressing her in dazzling white silk, radiant with holiness. And that is how husbands ought to love their wives. They're really doing themselves a favor—since they're already "one" in marriage. No one abuses his own body, does he? No, he feeds and pampers it. That's how Christ treats us, the church, since we are part of his body. And this is why a man leaves father and mother and cherishes his wife. No longer two, they become "one flesh." This is a huge mystery, and I don't pretend to understand it all. What is clearest to me is the way Christ treats the church. And this provides a good picture of how each husband is to treat his wife, loving himself in loving her, and how each wife is to honor her husband."

What I learned from all of these things is that it is wisdom to have marriage be held in honor by all. And in my heart, since marrying Dwight, I along with my husband, have tried to keep first things first by putting our marriage relationship as 2nd only in importance to our relationship to Jesus. This is a good thing. And it is wisdom.

Over the past few years, He's been showing me another facet of his perspective on marriage. Marriage needs to be held in honor among all because it's the closest representation of His relationship with His bride. And He is deeply & passionately in love with her.

3/12/06
Journal Entry:
5:05 am

The Lord woke me up. So I sat up in my bed. He then asked me to pray and wait upon Him. Then I got the following phrase: "Intimacy . . . You are calling for intimacy to Your bride."

7/1/08
Journal Entry:

Yesterday morning, I was lying in bed, waiting in silence. "Lord," I asked. "Do you want to show me anything? Is there something You want me to see or hear?" Suddenly, I saw the throne room. I was among many standing in front of Your throne and there You were sitting on your throne. All of sudden, You stood up and with total passion and yearning in Your heart. You reached out your scepter and cried out, "I yearn for my bride! I want my bride!" I felt & saw the yearning and passion in Your heart and I wanted to cry. Although I didn't weep, I was so deeply moved by Your love for her. I was amazed You longed for the church that much.

10/24/09
Journal Entry:

This morning, as I was soaking in the Lord's presence, I saw a pathway. I could only see Him in the distance, but He was dressed as a groom, and I could see Him holding her hands. I couldn't see the rest of the bride. Only her hands held in His. Then I heard Jesus saying His wedding vows to His bride, the church.

11/17/09
Journal Entry:

This morning, as I was waiting on the Lord, I covered my family with Your blood. Then I put on my armor. As I was getting ready to put on the mantle of humility, I noticed something above my head. I sensed it was some sort of covering. At first, I thought it was a mantle, a cloak of humility, but it wasn't. I got the cloak and put it on but the thing over my head was still there.

Then I realized what it was. It was a bridal veil. At first I had a really hard time with this. I sensed it represented the bride of Christ and her wedding veil was for a pure and spotless bride. Knowing my own sinful condition, I didn't feel worthy to wear it. He reminded me of His blood. Finally, He said, "Liza, look up." My head was hung low. I slowly raised my head and there He was, with His face smiling as He looked into my eyes. "Liza, will you do this for me?" How could I say no to my Jesus? "Okay Lord, I will wear it for you." Then the bridal veil was placed on my head. It had a crown that was silver, shiny, and loaded with sparkling gems (including diamonds) with tulle attached to it. What I then heard was "Crowned and purchased." Then the veil was covering me and the Lord spoke about His covering. I then saw Jesus grab a blanket. It was a white and blue striped blanket, and He put it around my shoulders. I felt so secure wrapped up in it. He explained to me that because I was crowned and purchased by His blood, I was covered by His covering and therefore I was protected and secure in Him.

2/10/11
Journal Entry:

I saw Jesus dressed in white riding His white horse. He was really BIG as was His horse! As he rode past me, He said, "I am passionate for My bride!" In the distance, I saw darkness. But in the midst of it, was a bright light. It was the light of His bride, the Church, and he was fiercely riding towards her, off His seat, leaning forward with His feet in the stirrups, intent on one purpose—to reach His bride.

———

After seeing His deep passion and His heart yearning to be with His bride, the church, I want His bride to be spotless, wrinkle free and ready to meet her bridegroom Jesus. And I want to start by focusing on my marriage. I want to honor my husband and to make marriage the 2nd most important relationship after Jesus, not just because we are commanded to do it, and not just because it brings Him glory, but because I now know how much He desires marriage to be held in honor. I love Him and want Him to see the fulfillment of his desire—to be one with His bride forever.

12/30/09

Journal Entry:

As I'm sitting here, pondering the importance of marriage, suddenly I hear the Lord speaking to my heart.

"Liza, remember Tiger Woods. He had it all, at least in the world's eyes. He had fame, power, riches, and what seemed to be the perfect family. But when the truth of the true nature of his marriage surfaced and his adulterous ways were exposed, even the world no longer deemed him a hero and someone worth following. I have placed in the hearts of people a desire to see marriage something worth honoring. So when the world sees your marriage, and they see unconditional love, respect, and honor—in their hearts, they know this is a good thing. They will see Me and will want what you have. I will use this to help draw the lost to myself. In these last days, I desire right alignment of hearts and relationships. My end time's army will be one where all those in it will hold marriage in honor. Make it your priority to respect, honor & love Dwight."

My personal prayer:

Jesus, help my marriage to be one that brings You honor & glory on Earth. Help me to love my husband, to respect him and to submit to his covering and authority as the head of our household. Please deepen my love, respect and passion for him. And help him to love me as You love the church. Teach him new ways of cherishing me. Keep our hearts and marriage free from any emotional and/or physical adultery. Protect our marriage from being out of alignment. May we never place each other above You. May we never place our children before each other or before You. May we never

place our ministry before You, each other & our children/
family. Help us always to keep first things first.
Thank you Jesus. For Your glory, for Your pleasure and in Your
name, amen.

Chapter 5
Kingdom Perspective on Children⸱
There is no junior Holy Spirit.

One of my favorite songs comes from Hillsong London. It is entitled "You are here." This is the chorus.

THE SAME POWER THAT CONQUERED THE GRAVE

LIVES IN ME, LIVES IN ME

YOUR LOVE THAT RESCUED THE EARTH

LIVES IN ME, LIVES IN ME

YOU ARE HERE

This means YOU (Jesus) are here, in my heart-in ME!

This is such a powerful truth!

One of the most powerful apostolic prayers that I know of comes from the Apostle Paul in Ephesians 1:19-23 (NLT). *"I also pray that you will understand the incredible greatness of God's power for us who believe him. This is the same mighty power that raised Christ from the dead and seated him in the place of honor at God's right hand in the heavenly realms. Now he is far above any ruler or authority or power or leader or anything else—not only in this world but also in the world to come. God has put all things under the authority of Christ and has made him head over all things for the benefit of the church. And the church is his body; it is made full and complete by*

Christ, who fills all things everywhere with himself." This verse became even more real to me in Nov. of 2008.

11/15/08
Journal Entry:

As we were worshiping at Elevate, we began to sing the song "You are here." Suddenly I saw a picture of our Elevate family as an army. Everyone was dressed in silver and black warrior outfits. They were lined up along the horizon for battle. Then the Lord spoke to my heart. "Liza, when you and the rest of Elevate really grasp and believe this truth in your hearts, that the same power that raised Jesus from the dead now lives inside of you, this is what you will become." Instantaneously, I watched as the whole line of soldiers began to charge forward, with weapons in their hands, banners flying in the sky, and fearless resolution in their eyes. It was a mighty army to behold.

———

Later, as I was writing this book, the Lord reminded me that this also applied to the children. There was and is no junior Holy Spirit! The same spirit that lived in me and other adult followers of Jesus, also lived in the children whose hearts received him with child-like faith.

Dwight and I have personally seen and experienced the power of the Holy Spirit through our 3 children. We wanted to share some of the kingdom perspectives He showed us through them with the following journal entries. Some of these experiences personally challenged our theology and we've had to throw out some religious mindsets that He exposed in us as we experienced these things. But we felt it was important to share these things because it demonstrated some of the new wine and new wineskins that He is using in these last days. I also talked to my children and asked them for their permission to share these stories with you. They all kindly agreed.

*Kingdom Perspective:
God can speak prophetically and powerfully through children, even when they are very young. He loves to show them His secrets.

9/02/2000
Journal Entry:

Kyla tonight really followed the janitor woman with her eyes and smiled as we entered the Food Court area. Later, as we were eating, Kyla again followed her with her eyes as she sat in the high chair. The woman walked past us and towards the tables across from us. Then Kyla stuck both her hands forward, towards the woman, and she began praying and interceding for her. Kyla looked sheepishly at me once and smiled, but she didn't put down her hands until she was done. Dwight and I both were amazed and filled with joy in her obedience to the Holy Spirit. Kyla is about 20 months old.

10/12/2000
Journal Entry:

Tonight, after we watched a powerful time of intercession for China on the television, Kyla came up to me. I was sitting on the floor. She put both hands on my hand and starting praying softly. Then she said, "Amen." Next, she laid her hands on my shoulders and prayed softly. Then she said, "Amen." Then she pointed to my eyes and said some words and ended with "Amen." Then she prayed with her hands on my head and said, "Amen." When she was done, she walked over to Dwight who was sitting on the couch next to me. She laid her hands on him, softly prayed for him and followed with "Amen." It sounded like she said the same prayer for both of us. The only word we recognized was "people." It was a word she had never said before. She's 21 ½ months old. We were so deeply touched by the Holy Spirit. Dwight and I both told the Lord out loud, "We receive whatever You want to impart to us through Kyla."

02/21/01
Journal Entry:

Kyla woke up at 3:30 a.m. this morning. I had a prayer time at 5 a.m. with my prayer buddy Cindy at our church. After I nursed her, I found Kyla still awake. She wanted to hug me so she wrapped her arms around me. Immediately, I sensed that she wanted to minister and impart God's anointing to me because this morning's prayer time was special. We were going to pray in our new prayer room at our church for the first time and we wanted to seek His will regarding the prayer ministry. I told the Lord, "I receive all that You want to impart to me through Kyla." A few minutes later, Kyla unwrapped her arms, looked at me, smiled and said, "Remember, worship." I was floored. It was a word from the Lord. I wasn't planning to take my guitar or music, but immediately I knew that Cindy waand I needed to worship God this morning in that prayer room and I needed to take my guitar and music with me. Kyla then rewrapped her arms around me and hugged me for 30 more minutes. Then at 4:23 a.m. she rolled over and went back to sleep. I felt the peace and presence of God the entire time she hugged me. What an awesome experience! Kyla is 26 months old.

9/02/01
Journal Entry:

Early this morning, Kyla woke up at 3 a.m. crying. She had a fever. She stayed up for 2 more hours. Boy was I tired!!! We had a special church gathering at 10 a.m. at a bandstand in our city. I prayed "Lord, if You want us to go, please help Kyla to wake up happy and wanting to go to church. At 9:25 a.m. Kyla woke up happy and said, "Mommy, let's go to church!" I was amazed. She had no fever but she still had a bit of a runny nose. I was hesitant. "Lord", I cried out silently, "do You still want us to go?" I then sat down to put on Kyla's shoes but in my heart, I was still hesitant. Kyla suddenly looked at me and said, "Mommy, God is bigger." With eyes wide opened, I turned to her and asked if she felt well to go to church. Kyla nodded and said, "Yes." As I started driving Kyla (almost 3 yrs. old) and my son Kairos (4 ½ months old) through the pouring rain, I silently spoke the following phrase in my mind. "Am I crazy God? Should I have allowed Kyla to go out today in this kind of weather?" Immediately, Kyla spoke out from the backseat. "Mommy, don't be afraid!" I was floored!!!! I didn't speak any of these things out loud. Yet God showed her what I needed to hear. Thank you God for speaking to me through my daughter.

2/03/02
Journal Entry:

For the past 2-3 weeks, Kyla shared dreams that she had with me. "What was your dream about?" I'd ask. "God and Jesus! Happy!!" she'd reply.

Another morning, Kyla was sobbing tears as she woke up. I asked Kyla what was the matter. She replied, "Mommy . . . Jesus . . . cross . . . die . . . Kyla cry . . . Kyla sad." I started weeping as she shared this with me. Kyla looked at me and asked, "Is mommy sad too?" Tears rolled down her face as she sobbed. Shocked at what she had just told me, I tried to answer her as my heart ached to comfort her. "Jesus died on the cross, but He rose from the dead after that." Kyla's sad eyes showed me that she didn't comprehend what I was saying. I didn't know what else to say or do. She remained sad, brokenhearted and mournful and my heart cried out to God. "Show her the victory over death!! Reveal to her the resurrection."

Her naptime came up that day, and when she awoke, Kyla had a huge smile. She ran to me and said, "Mommy! Jesus alive! Kyla happy!" I was relieved. "Wow Kyla. Yes, Jesus is alive! He rose from the dead!" I replied. This time Kyla nodded in agreement. Her young 3-year-old heart supernaturally understood, by the grace of God, the resurrection of Jesus Christ! I was in awe of God's goodness to her.

One week later, Kyla awoke one morning having had another dream. "Mommy, I had dream about God and Jesus!" "Was it happy?" I asked. "Yes, happy. Jesus is coming soon." I was floored, not expecting her to say this. "Wow!" I responded. "Really?" Kyla replied very matter of fact back to me. "Yes, He's coming soon. Jesus wanted to play with me. We had fun. We sang "La, La, La, La, La, La La" (a line from a worship song we sang as a family together). He was wearing white and blue."

2/07/02
Journal Entry:
Tonight, Kyla pointed to my chest and said, "Treasure." I pointed to my gold necklace. "Is this the treasure?" Kyla

responded "No." Then she pointed to my chest, put her fingertips on top and then proclaimed, "The treasure in here", as she patted my heart. I felt deeply encouraged and touched by her words of life. This totally touched my heart. We hugged and cuddled on the couch. It was a special memory to me.

4/02/02
Journal Entry:

I had the most awesome talk with Kyla tonight. (Kyla is now almost 3 ½ yrs. old.) After we had just prayed as a family with her on her bed and as Dwight and I were leaving the room, Kyla said, "Mommy, stay with me." "No", I replied, "you need to go to sleep by yourself." "NO!" Kyla staunchly retorted. "Kyla, you won't be alone. God is with you." "No," Kyla said. "God is outside." "Kyla, God is inside. You have a heart inside of you." "No" said Kyla. "I don't have a heart."

"Yes," I replied. "You have a heart inside of you. You just can't see it. Remember the town we built? Remember the Kyla Periwinkle Hotel? We put your Minnie Mouse plush toy inside of the hotel. Once we covered Minnie up, could you see her from the outside?" Kyla paused. "No, you couldn't see Minnie but she was still inside. In the same way, you have a heart inside of you. You can't see it, just like Minnie Mouse in the hotel, but it's still there. Remember the video we saw? Jesus was standing outside of your heart. He wants to come in so He can be inside your heart forever. But you need to let him in. Do you want Jesus to come into your heart?" With a serious look, Kyla nodded and said, "Yes." "Okay Kyla, then tell him. Ask Him to come inside your heart." Kyla then turned to look up at the ceiling and said these simple words. "Jesus, come into my heart." I wept silently, happily stunned by this

29

spontaneous moment. "Kyla, let's pray." Dear Jesus" I began. "Thank you for coming into Kyla's heart. Thank you that you'll be with Kyla forever and that she'll be with you forever. Amen." Kyla then looked at me with delight and surprise. "Mommy, I can hear God talking to me. I have Jesus in my heart!" Stunned, I somehow calmly replied, "Kyla, Mommy's going to go." "Okay." Before turning away, I asked out of curiosity, "Is God still talking to you?" "Ahh ha." "Have a good time with God Kyla. Don't forget to listen." Kyla looked away at the ceiling then looked at me. "Okay mommy." Then she quickly turned away from me to her side, facing the wall. I left with tears streaming down my cheeks. I ran to our bedroom as I excitedly cried out, "Dwight!" Then I happily shared with him this miraculous moment.

Later as I prayed, I got 2 verses from the Lord. He redirected my thoughts to verses He had given me after Koby died and before we had conceived Kyla. (Genesis 22 and Deuteronomy 6:4-25) What a glorious day!

4/08/06
Journal Entry:

I had to lead worship at a women's dinner. Kyla came along. As I was driving home, I was happily surprised to hear Kyla share with me that she saw Jesus standing next to me as the women began to worship Him with the first song. She then saw a multitude of angels appear that began to dance and worship Him with us as we sang "How Great is our God." She didn't see them after that first song but she shared how she felt His presence throughout. Later, as I sat in quietness on my knees before Him in the stillness of the late night hour, I heard Him speak to my heart. "I'm here, standing next to you." I opened my physical eyes and saw nothing but I chose to believe. Then the room began to pulsate with waves of light falling from the sky. "Pretty cool!" I thought. Then it was quiet again and the pulsating waves of light were gone. But He spoke again to my heart. "There isn't much time left. I am coming soon . . . much sooner than you think. Don't waste time. Time is more precious than gold."

4/09/06
Journal Entry:
Driving in the car to Taco Bell. Kyla saw an opening in the sky. Through that opening, she saw Jesus on a while horse with other angels in chariots riding around. Kyla was told by the Lord "It's a practice run!" She described Jesus' horse as huge and extremely powerful—stronger than an SUV!

11/14/06
Journal Entry:
What a special time with Jesus and Kyla. Lying in the bedroom, waiting on the Lord, I could see bright lights fill the room and I could feel His presence. Then Kyla came into the room, crawled into bed and laid next to me. Eventually we looked up at the ceiling together and waited on God. It was so cool because we both got to see the same things—the same colors & lights. Then Kyla said, "Hey, is there a hole in the ceiling? Do you see that?" I just laughed as I saw the familiar open hole in the ceiling. "Mom, it looks like the dark night outside—dark blue sky with stars in it." I just laughed with delight as we both saw the bright lights. Later, at 1:30 a.m., I was lying with Kyla in her room. Kyla said "Come on Mom. Let's wait on God." So we did. As we looked up at the ceiling and waited, we saw lights and colors and then we saw the open hole in the ceiling. All I saw was a hole in the ceiling with the blue night sky. Then Kyla began to describe what she saw through that

hole. "Mom, I see the Holy City—the beautiful buildings and the streets of gold. It is so glorious. Now I see a desert and then a beautiful valley with streams in it. Mom, I can even hear it. It's so peaceful! I can hear the birds singing. Now I see a pasture. It's really pretty green. There's beautiful flowers in it—yellow and pink in color—and I see white picket fences." I was thrilled to hear what she was seeing. All I saw was bright light coming through the opening. It was glorious!

12/12/06
Journal Entry:

We were eating breakfast when all of a sudden, Kailee (2 years old) saw an angel. No one else could see it. Kailee suddenly brightened up, pointed to the ceiling and said, "Look! Angel!" Then she smiled and waved to the angel. I couldn't see it but I could feel the presence of God.

12/22/06
Journal Entry:

In the morning, during breakfast, Kyla (8 years old) started asking questions about abortion. It was a very deep talk. Then Kyla felt impressed to spend more time with God so she did. Then she wanted her siblings to join her. As I sat at my desk, working on Christmas presents, I could hear Kyla interceding her heart out for the nations. In her room, I could hear her leading her siblings in worship, praise and declarations. She yelled out, "God, have mercy on America!" I was so deeply touched. That night, as I lay Kairos down to sleep, he started asking questions about why he couldn't hear God's voice. So I asked him if he wanted more of Jesus and if he wanted to ask Him for help to hear His voice. Kairos said, "Yes." So we prayed together. "Jesus, please fill and baptize Kairos with Your Spirit." The next morning, after the kids spent time with the Lord, I asked Kairos if he heard Jesus. He nodded "yes" and said, "I heard Him in my heart." Thank you Lord!

6/8/07
Journal Entry:

A couple of nights ago, I was lying on the bottom bunk of the children's bed with Kailee (2 years, 8 months old). It was bedtime. All of a sudden, Kailee turned towards me and propped herself up a bit. As she stared into my eyes, she gave me a huge smile and said, "God loves you!" I smiled back at her in silence. Then she got a little more intense. "Mommy, God loves you!" she declared with urgency. Immediately, I sensed it was God speaking through her to encourage my heart. "MOMMY, GOD LOVES YOU!" I started to get teary eyed as the truth of these few words started to finally hit my heart. Kailee kept repeating herself and only stopped once she sensed I really got it-that Jesus truly loved me and that I received this truth in my heart. What an amazing thing to be ministered to so powerfully through a 2 year old. Thank you Jesus!

6/10/07
Journal Entry:

(Kyla sketched out what she saw)

Kyla and I were lying down, waiting on the Lord at night before going to sleep. All of sudden, Kyla saw a huge opening in the ceiling. In it, she saw a huge gem, about 4 feet long and 1 foot wide. She also saw rainbow colors and angels dancing around it. "Mom, it's a huge diamond! Mom, Jesus just told me this huge diamond is you. He loves you so much. This is what you are to him. Mommy, I'm so proud of you. I have happy tears too. Mom, you will be going to many nations and meeting children with new languages. Mom, we're diamonds too. And as we minister, these children will become diamonds too."

Then Kyla saw a 2nd vision of a huge rainbow. The rainbow turned and became a hollow tunnel. She saw 5 homeless children wearing ragged clothing. It was rainy and cold outside. The children came inside and there were all sorts of food on a table. There was a TV and beds for them to sleep in.

Jesus then told Kyla that the rainbow was Elevate. The cold rain was the devil's fiery weapon(s) and the children were people in the future we'd meet. Kyla said that when they would meet us and go to Elevate, their lives would be supernaturally changed forever. The children represented adults too.

Then Kyla got a 3rd vision. She saw huge hands—the hands of Jesus. In his hands was a huge treasure box, about 5 feet long and 4 feet tall. It was locked and covered in gold. Then she saw Jesus open the treasure box. Kyla could see gold, fruit of the Spirit, gems, jewels, and jewelry-all kinds of treasure in the box. Then Kyla told me to hold both hands open. So I did. Then she saw Jesus dump all the treasure out of the chest and into my hands. Then she directed me to put 1 hand on my head, and 1 on my heart and receive it all. So I did. I felt the power of God hit me as I received this beautiful gift in faith. Thank you Lord for your goodness. And thank you for Kyla.

1/17/08
Journal Entry:

I was having a discouraging day. It was just Kailee and I together at lunch. The clock read 2:20 p.m. I put my head down as I told Kailee, "Mommy needs to talk to Jesus." Kailee looked at me (now 3) and said, "Oh—okay." All of a sudden, she said, "Mommy, look! It's Jesus! He's walking over to you. Jesus is here." I looked up. "Where?" "Mommy, he's now right here, next to you." As she said this, she pointed next to me. "Is he smiling?" I asked. "Umm . . . . no", she replied, as she looked up next to me. "Kailee, does he look like this?" I asked as I made a concerned face. Kailee looked again. "Mommy, now he is smiling." I felt relieved. Tears flowed down my cheeks as I was deeply moved that Jesus himself was here to comfort me. I really had a tough day with 3 young kids. So I sat with my head down on the table, tears flowing freely as I poured my heart out to him. Kailee then spoke up. "Mommy, Jesus said, 'Don't worry . . . (then she paused for a brief moment, looking over next to me) and then said, " . . . Liza." I could tell she was feeling uncomfortable calling me by my first name, but after she said that, she gave me the biggest smile. I was floored because I knew that it was God telling her to tell me this. I wept happy tears. It ended up being a great day!

3/18/08
Journal Entry:

Today as the kids prayed over me, Kailee (now 3 yrs. old) told me to take the gift Jesus had for me. With her hand held open, she said it was a pink shell with lips. Kyla (now 9) looked at her lil' sister's open hand and said she saw it as lip gloss. I couldn't see anything with my natural eye. But sensing this was the Lord, I took the gift from Kailee and put it on my lips. "How does it look?" Kailee looked at my lips and with a smile replied, "Pretty in pink and shiny!!!" Immediately the Lord spoke to my heart. He was covering my lips with grace. Kyla got a word from the Lord and spoke it to me. "Be quick to think but slow to speak." I was both convicted and humbled because that week I had been impatient and quick with my mouth with my children at home. Thank you Jesus.

1/1/09
Journal Entry:
(The Lord showed me some things of which I will share later in this book on this particular day.)

But at the end of my time with Jesus on New Year's Day, I suddenly I saw myself with huge dumbo looking ears. It was kind of funny! Jesus then told me, "I am making you into a good listener, to listen with great clarity. In 2009, you will shine . . . Me!"

1/13/09
Journal Entry:

Yesterday, Kailee (then 4 years old) and I were sitting in the kitchen. Kailee looked at me and said, "Mommy, you have good listening ears. Jesus told me to look at your ears." At that instant, her little almond shaped eyes shifted to my ears. Then with a smile, her eyes shifted back to gaze into mine. "He said, 'Your mommy has good listening ears!" I was astonished but delighted. Thank you Jesus for confirming what you told me on January 1st through Kailee!

11/2010
Journal Entry

Kailee (recently turned 6 years old) felt a song on her heart so she asked me to write down the words of what she was going to sing. This is her song, as best as I could write down the lyrics as she sang. I pray it would bless your heart. It did mine. It was beautiful and heartfelt. I just wish I could have recorded the melody as she sang this new song.

Kailee's New Song:

As sunflowers grow into the ground, how they bloom outside
How beautiful they are LORD, I love you.

What the LORD seeks in your heart (?)

You died for us
You're my everything

God made this Earth and we live in it
Amazing love . . .
Sunflowers grow upon the ground, to grow like You.

You're my King of Heaven
You are exciting
Happiness, joy to the world

As we sing, we see each other as we are
We are family
I cannot hate you because we are family
I can't attack you because you're family

God is bringing the LORD (?)
He loves the world
God made this world
He made the flowers
He made the trees and shade
He made me

He knew me, me and my family
He is the glory
He's my glory
He's my Dad

He is the only home I have
I'm blessed by my dad & mom and my King of hearts

Rock-a-bye baby
Baby Jesus
He grew up into a great man
But before that He was a kid, then a teenager
and then a man
Then He died on the cross
Then God turned to His son
He made a big earthquake
He died and forgave
He died and rose again
He sure did

And He went up to heaven and His kingdom

If my people would know and seek His eyes
And seek Him more
Send Your angels and Your joy falls on us
We need everything He has for us
Oh lead me to the cross
He died and rose again . . .

1/31/10
Journal Entry:

Yesterday morning, Kailee woke up really early. She came to my bedroom and had already changed out of her pajamas. Kailee is 6. As I got out of bed, I saw that she had already cleaned and made her bed and cleaned her desk. I was shocked! The past few weeks had been the hardest I've had with her since she was born. Every day had been a battle of the wills and she had chosen to be stubborn and rebellious. I had been praying my heart out to the Lord, crying out to Him to please change Kailee's heart and to please deal with her because I was frankly at the end of my rope.

As I asked her why she was up so early, I was touched as she humbly explained that the Lord woke her up early. This is what she shared with me as she explained her time with Jesus.

"Kailee." "Jesus? Is that You?" "Yes Kailee, it's Me. Can I talk with you for a few minutes?"

"Sure Jesus." At that point, Kailee shared how she sat up in her bed and listened. "Kailee, you have been walking on the dark side. And you need to stop. You need to walk on the bright side."

Kailee then shared how Jesus told her she needed to listen to her parents, to make her bed, to clean her room, and so on. She explained to me that she told Jesus she was going to choose the bright side from now on. I was thrilled!

That whole day, Dwight and I were in awe as we saw the supernatural change in her heart. Everything the Lord asked her to do, including making her brother's bed, cleaning mommy's desk, and so on, she did in obedience to Him. She listened so sweetly and quickly when I asked her to do things like brush her teeth or to come to me. And we saw God's wonderful fruit of the Spirit flowing in and through her.

That night, as I lay in Kailee's bed with her before she went to sleep, I really felt the Lord wanted to speak to her. At first when I asked if she sensed Jesus wanted to speak to her, she said she saw and heard nothing. I asked the Lord about it and again really felt that He wanted to speak to her. She sweetly agreed to ask Jesus about it so she said out loud, "Jesus? Jesus?" And she waited. Then she started to speak. I was caught off guard because I was expecting Kailee to share something just for her, but the words she heard and spoke out loud was for both of us. She talked about our hearts being pure & full of love and that Jesus was so pleased with both of us. My heart was deeply touched. What an encouraging thing to hear a word from the Lord through your own children.

3/15/11
Journal Entry:

This morning I spent time soaking in the presence of God with Kairos. My son then turned to me and said, "Jesus told me to tell you that you have a kind heart. You are kind to others. Jesus loves you. And I love Jesus."

3/27/11
Journal Entry:

Last night at Walmart, Kailee smashed her finger. She was crying. Kairos prayed for her finger. Immediately the pain went away. Jesus healed her.

1/7/12
Journal Entry:

At Elevate, we all spent time being still before the Lord, including the children. This is what Kailee got.

She saw herself in a boat with other people in water. She saw Jesus walking on the water. He held out His hands to her as He said, "Come and walk on the water." The others in the boat started to put her down. They told her she couldn't do it. That's when Jesus told her "No matter what anyone else says, you CAN do it because I said you can." So Kailee chose to believe Him. She got out of the boat and she walked on the water to Jesus.

Kingdom Perspective:
The KEY of DESPERATION
draws one closer to Jesus.

3/28/06
Journal Entry:

Today Kyla, our oldest child (now 7), had been totally attacked by the enemy, for no apparent reason. She's been attacked in her mind by thoughts of fear such that she's in tears and literally shaking. Jesus help us!

3/30/06
Journal Entry:

Kyla continues to pray and devour the word of God since Tuesday night (3/28) when a spirit of fear began to heavily attack her. She couldn't sleep at night and couldn't eat. Yesterday, as she devoured the bible, underlining scripture and praying, she later shared what Jesus told her regarding her whole ordeal. "Mom, God told me why I am going through all this. I had too much pride and He is teaching me that it is all about HIM—His strength, His power, His glory." I was amazed. (Kyla is 7 years old.)

3/31/06
Journal Entry:

Today was an amazing day! It started off typical—my 3 kids testing my patience, me raising my voice, etc. Kyla read her bible and then started school. Later, she sat on our long sofa, reading a geography book when all of a sudden she exclaimed, "Mom! Oh my goodness!" I glanced over to her from my desk about 3 feet away. With excitement, she exclaimed, "God just gave me a vision of Jesus! I got to see Him!" "What?" I gasped as my eyes welled with tears. "God gave you a vision of Jesus?" "Yes, mommy." Then with a huge smile, she proclaimed, "Mommy, Jesus is standing right next to me." I just started laughing incredulously (although my eyes saw nothing in the natural as I scanned the area next to her). It's as if my child read my mind as she immediately replied, "Mom, I have my spiritual eyes on, not like the fleshly ones I used to use. That's why I can see Him. Mommy, God wants you to see Him and He wants to talk to you too if you'll just let Him. Come on Mommy!"

I got out of my chair and sat down on the short sofa across her. "Mommy, you can see Jesus and hear God too." Then she paused, took and a breath and said, "But mommy, you have to read His Word, the bible and when you read it the way I have been doing these days in desperation, you'll hear Him too." Then Kyla started laughing. "Mommy, Jesus is reading this book to me." Happy tears began to flow down her face as she wept. I wept too. "You know mommy, Jesus said that when He saw how scared I was, He wanted to comfort me so He asked His father and God the Father gave Him permission to stay with me at my house.

Kyla then continued to read her geography book. All of a sudden she giggled. "Mommy, Jesus is laughing!" "Why?" I asked. "He was reading the part in the book when people thought the Earth was flat." Kyla read on. "Mommy, Jesus is singing a line from a song. No wait. Jesus just told me it is the Holy Spirit who is singing. Mommy, you know this morning when you were getting all stressed out and raising your voice? Jesus was right by you, telling you to calm down, and to be gentler with your words."

Conviction pierced my heart. I cried and said out loud, "I repent!" Kyla giggled. "Mommy, He forgives you."

Kyla continued. "Mommy, Jesus said He's going to stay with me, play with me, eat with me, sleep with me until I go to heaven. He's staying with our family. Mommy, God said come to Him and ask Him when you don't know what to do. When you have questions, ask Him. Call upon Him. He'll speak to you and show you but you need to read His Word." I kept weeping—feeling incredulous, happy and convicted all at the same time.

4/3/06
Journal Entry:
Kyla shared a song the Holy Spirit put into her heart. I got to hear this beautiful new song one day as I drove Kyla in the car. She was in the back seat singing this song to Jesus.

EVERMORE

Verse 1:
I would have not made it without you (repeat 3x)

Chorus:
And I will love you evermore (repeat 7x)

Verse 2:
I love you Jesus (repeat 2x and v. 1)

Kingdom Perspective:
God is speaking prophetically through children.
Will we have the ears to hear what He is saying in this hour through them?

3/15/07
Journal Entry:
1 a.m.
(The Parable of the Sower as seen through the eyes of an 8-½ year old)

I spent time with Kyla tonight. Then we waited on the Lord in silence and He gave her the following vision.

First she saw flowers, including white dandelions and flowers in all shades of purple. Then Kyla saw one flower close up on a tree. It was purple. She watched it open and then saw another purple shoot/flower within it. Next, Kyla saw a hand picking the flower. It was Jesus picking up the purple flower. Right after that, she saw Jesus standing by the flowers. They were along a road. He picked up a bunch of flowers. The rest died along the road or had grasshoppers eat them up. Jesus then took the flowers in His hands and planted them further down in a place with good soil where the flowers started to grow really well.

Then she saw Jesus walk over to some flowers growing in rocks. He picked them. They didn't have a lot of roots. But once He picked them, all the rest of the flowers/dandelions in that area turned black or got eaten by grasshoppers. Jesus took those flowers that He picked and planted them in the good soil.

Next, Jesus walked over to a place where there were weeds. She saw black colored weeds, various shades of gray colored weeds and brown weeds. Then she saw 5 plants with flowers among the weeds. The weeds were trying really hard to choke them up. Jesus came over and picked up those 5 plants. Their roots grew really strong even in his hands. Then He walked over and planted them in the good soil.

Then He had a basket filled with flowers of all sorts of colors—red, blue, green, yellow, orange, indigo. He started picking the purple flowers and putting them into His basket. There were a few flowers He had to throw out of His basket—a black plant and a grey plant (the plant was completely black or grey, including the color of the leaves, the stalk, etc). There were some black flowers, some brown flowers and some grey flowers in His basket but these were okay. Only the flowers were those colors but the rest of those plants were green.

Then Jesus walked over to the rocky place. He started picking up all the rocks and threw them out. Then He put good soil in that place and planted flowers and they all started growing well.

Then there was a hammock and hammock chair. Jesus was sitting in the hammock. There was also a castle made out of stone and glass. It started to rain. With the rain, the flowers started to grow really big. Then out of the castle came an old man. It was the Heavenly Father. He was smiling.

After Kyla shared all that she saw moment by moment with me, there came a moment of silence. What was the revelation of what she saw? Then Kyla shared that she didn't know where this came from in the bible but the words that came to her were: "You reap what you sow. You sow what you reap."

Then she continued to wait. Then she got another vision. In it were people that were all dark black, except for the white of their eyes. They came to the roadside and started planting seeds. They had some dandelion seeds and started planting them every where—along the road, along the rocks and along the weedy areas—but they didn't touch the good soil. Then she shared the following message. "Time is short. Every second counts. Once a second passes, it can never be lived again. People think they are planting good seeds but they will be surprised because some of the seeds are junk seed. You reap what you sow. You can never get this day again. You can never get this year again. You can't go back to 1998 and then to 2018 and come back to 2007. Time is running out. You reap what you sow. Sow what you reap."

Then she stopped, looked into my eyes intently and then said, "Message from Jesus. 'I love you Liza. And I always will.'"

12/23/07
Journal Entry:

We were on Oahu for Christmas and staying at Dad Kobayashi's house. We were all lying down on folding mattresses in the middle of the living room. It was past midnight and as we prayed as a family, Kyla had a vision.

First she saw a beautiful, translucent cross appear before her. "Mommy, it's glorious—so beautiful. There are diamonds on it and it is made out of clear gold. Glory is emanating from it. In the middle of the cross is a red stone in the shape of a heart. I see pictures of different states, flags of different nations, pictures of people of all ages all around the cross. Now all the pictures are being sucked into the red heart of the cross. Oh . . . mom.

46

There's another cross. It's a silly cross. It is made out of rocks. Now that silly cross just crumbled into a heap of rocks.

Now there are paths in front of these crosses. The beautiful cross has a narrow path in front of it. The silly cross has a wide path in front of it. Now the scene is moving and the crosses are moving farther back. There are rivers of water in front of the crosses. One river is narrow (from the beautiful, glorious cross) and the other is wide (from the silly cross). At the bottom of these rivers were boats—rowboats (for the thin, translucent cross) and a huge ferry (for the silly cross). Most people boarded the ferry. Few got into the rowboats. Those that did rowed to the thin cross. Once there, they got out and the rowboats returned to the bottom where others got in and rowed back to the beautiful cross. The ferry carried the people up to the silly cross. Once there, they got out too. Then the ferry returned to the bottom to pick up more people.

Along each path, there were places where the path forked—one to a place of food, the other to the path leading to a cross. I see people on the narrow path stopping to eat, then returning to their journey. On the broad path, people stopped for food. Some people, after eating the food, found a path to the beautiful cross and eventually made it there. Others returned to the broad path and made their way to the silly cross.

Later, I asked the Lord about this. He said that because heart motives aren't right, people will find themselves on the path to the wrong cross. Their reasons for serving Jesus wasn't for His glory—but for their own. He said, **"If the One Thing isn't purely Me, then it's not for me."**

Chapter 6
The Power of the Blood of Jesus

I'd like to share a short scenario with you. I'd like you to imagine Jesus sitting on His throne about 20 feet away from you. What would your response be if He beckoned you to come forward to Him? Would you shrink back from His presence in shame and regret? Would you stay frozen where you were trapped by indecisiveness? Or would you approach Him? If you approached Him, would it be with confidence? If yes, would it be with self-confidence or God confidence?

I'm sorry for the barrage of questions, but let me explain why I asked these things.

Growing up, I had a mom with whom I felt I was never good enough. She was a good mom. But no matter how hard I tried to do well in school, be an honor roll student, excel in my studies, be a student officer, etc, it never seemed to be good enough for her. As an adult, I now understand that part of why my mom treated me this way was because she grew up in a very harsh and conditional love upbringing with her father. It was also because of the insecurity and shame she felt and experienced because of mental illness. I love my mom. I've forgiven her and I'm still praying for her total healing and deliverance. But because of the conditional love I received from her, what happened next was that I started basing my self-esteem and my identity as a follower of Jesus <u>on my performance</u> as a Christian and **not** on God's unconditional love, grace & undeserved mercy because of the cross and

His sacrifice. As I became an adult, this affected the way I would come to Jesus.

When I was growing in the Lord and doing well in my walk (spending time in His Word, praying and serving Him), I would feel I could come to Him and approach His throne with confidence. But what I didn't realize was that I was approaching Jesus out of **self**-confidence. There is a huge difference between self-confidence and God confidence. At that time, I didn't know this.

Then when I was in sin or struggling with some inner battle, I wouldn't approach Him because I felt so unworthy. I felt I didn't deserve His love and thus felt I couldn't come to Him. I was also afraid of God, believing that if I got close to Him, I would be severely disciplined by Him because I believed He would be angry with me because He was such a holy God and I wasn't being very holy in my actions. This perspective I had of God was warped because this lack of confidence was based in false humility and also in a lack of understanding His true nature and the depths of His unconditional love. I also didn't understand, believe and fully receive His grace that He freely gave because of His sacrifice on the cross.

The bible also says in Hebrews 4:15-16 (NASB)—*"For we do not have a high priest who cannot sympathize with our weaknesses, but One who has been tempted in all things as we are, yet without sin. Therefore <u>let us draw near with confidence to the throne of grace</u>, so that we may receive mercy and find grace to help in time of need."*

I personally had a very difficult time with the part underlined above. As I struggled between self-confidence (pride) in approaching His throne of grace and false humility (pride) in staying as far away from His throne of grace when I spiritually blew it, I prayed and asked the Lord to help me draw near to Him with God confidence to His throne of grace. He then led me to Hebrews 10:35-36 (ESV). *"Therefore do not throw away your confidence, which has a great reward. For you have need of endurance, so that when you have done the will of God you may receive what is promised."*

I remember asking Jesus this question when He led me to this verse. "Lord, what do you mean by confidence?" Immediately, He led me to the following verses.

*Romans 5:8-11 (ESV)
But God shows his love for us in that while we were still sinners, Christ died for us. Since, <u>therefore, we have now been justified by his blood</u>, much more shall we be saved by him from the wrath of God. For if while we were enemies we were reconciled to God by the death of his Son, much more, now that we are reconciled, shall we be saved by his life. More than that, we also rejoice in God through our Lord Jesus Christ, through whom we have now received reconciliation.

*Hebrews 10:10-(ESV)
And by that will, <u>we have been sanctified through the offering of the body of Jesus Christ once for all</u>.

*Hebrews 10:19-25(ESV)
Therefore, brothers, since <u>we have confidence to enter the holy places by the blood of Jesus</u>, by the new and living way that he opened for us through the curtain, that is, through his flesh, and since we have a great priest over the house of God, ˡᵉᵗ us draw near with a true heart in full assurance of faith, with our hearts sprinkled clean from an evil conscience and our bodies washed with pure water. Let us hold fast the confession of our hope without wavering, for he who

promised is faithful. And let us consider how to stir up one another to love and good works, not neglecting to meet together, as is the habit of some, but encouraging one another, and all the more as you see the Day drawing near.

Wow! **My confidence** to enter the holy places and to approach His throne of grace **was <u>in the blood of Jesus</u>—not myself!** What powerful, revelatory truth! That means I can approach and go to Jesus at any time, whether I am at my highest high, or my lowest low. He loves me and His blood has made me totally valued. I am of priceless worth because His blood covers me. My sins, past, present and even future, have been paid for by Jesus and His sacrifice on the cross.

As I pondered why these particular scriptures, which I know I had read and had at least memorized Romans 5:8 and Hebrews 4:16 as a teenager, hit me so hard this time around, I finally realized something about the difference between my mind and my heart. My mind knew these verses and even had them memorized. But many times, my heart didn't "**<u>know</u>**" this truth. At times, there was a super long distance between my mind and my heart. What I began to realize was that there was a huge difference between relating to God just with your mind (intellectually) versus relating to him with your heart.

God created our minds to process information, which is great. The mind is important. But it is limited. With more information, our minds will always ask more questions. Yes, it is good to ask God questions. He loves it when we spend time with Him and ask. But if we choose to relate to God mainly through our minds first, we will find ourselves totally unprepared for the increasing difficult and dark times that are to come. Why? **Because God will not always explain Himself.** And even if he did, it will be way more than we could humanly ever comprehend.

Isaiah 55:8-10 (NIV) states, *"For my thoughts are not your thoughts, neither are your ways my ways," declares the LORD. As the heavens are higher than the earth, so are my ways higher than your ways and my thoughts than your thoughts."*

When my son Koby died, I didn't really receive an answer or explanation to why he died. To be more specific, my mind didn't get a thorough explanation for his death from God. But my heart got it. I felt His peace and His assurance that for whatever reason, his death on Earth brought more glory to Jesus then if my son was allowed to live. And because my heart heard His voice, my heart, soul and spirit were covered with His peace and healing and victory flowed—even though my mind didn't fully understand or get the answers it wanted.

This may seem like a silly question, but when I think back to when I first started my own personal relationship with Jesus and I asked Him into my life, did I invite him into my mind? No. I invited Him into my heart. It was in my heart where His Holy Spirit came to live inside of me. The same is true for you. The heart was created and designed by God to receive and respond to revelation.

In John 17:3 (NASB), it states: "This is eternal life, that they may <u>know</u> You, the only true God, and Jesus Christ whom You have sent."

The Greek word for know is "ginosko." It means to learn to know, come to know, get a knowledge of, perceive, recognize, understand, or to understand completely. It refers to knowing Jesus in our innermost being which is in our hearts. In the New Testament, ginosko frequently indicates a relationship between the person "knowing" and the object known. In this respect, what is "known" is of value or importance to the one who knows, and hence the establishment of the relationship.

Ginosko also refers to knowing by experience, implying a process through a growing relationship with Jesus of knowing Him here, in our hearts.

This same word is also found in the following verses:

Ephesians 3:19 (NASB)
*And to **know** the love of Christ which surpasses knowledge,*
that you may be filled up to all the fullness of God.
John 8:32 (NASB)
*And you will **know** the truth, and the truth will make you free."*
John 10:14 (NASB)
*"I am the good shepherd, and I **know** My own and My own*
know Me,
Philippians 3:10 (NASB)
*That I may **know** Him and the power of His resurrection*
and the fellowship of His sufferings, being conformed to His death;

Let these verses go deep into your heart. These verses aren't referring to knowing Him with simply head knowledge. This is eternal life, that we **KNOW HIM**! For me personally, I used to think of eternal life simply as what I would get to experience once I died and left this planet. Yet, John 17:3 states that eternal life is to know God. We can experience eternal life NOW! What powerful truth!

In Ephesians 1:16-20 (ESV), it also talks about "knowing" God.

"I do not cease to give thanks for you, remembering you in my prayers, that the God of our Lord Jesus Christ, the

Father of glory, may give you the Spirit of wisdom and of revelation in the knowledge of him, having the eyes of your hearts enlightened, that you may __know__ what is the hope to which he has called you, what are the riches of his glorious inheritance in the saints, and what is the immeasurable greatness of his power toward us who believe, according to the working of his great might that he worked in Christ when he raised him from the dead and seated him at his right hand in the heavenly places,"

In these verses, the word "know" in bold is a Greek word—eido/oida. (to see in present tense) In this case, it's not so much about what is known by experience but rather, by a revelation and insight that the Holy Spirit gives that is drilled into one's heart. Isn't that awesome?

There is a difference between believing with our minds and believing with our hearts. We may well know and believe in our minds that Jesus is now above all rule and authority and dominion, but if we really believed this in our hearts, our lives would be radically different.

In *Romans 10:10 (ESV), it says, "for with the **heart** one believes & is justified."*

We need to know Jesus deep in here—in our hearts. That is eternal life. When God speaks to us from His heart, He isn't looking for a mental assent but a heart response from us. God desires and created us to relate to him—***heart to heart***.

2 Chronicles 16:9(NIV) says, *"For the eyes of the LORD range throughout the earth to strengthen those whose **hearts** are fully committed to him.*

Please hear me. I'm not saying throw out your mind. But rather that the foundation of your relationship to Jesus has to start inside here—in your heart. In my marriage to Dwight, our relationship is not based on relating to each other simply mind to mind trying to figure each other out all the time. We love each other and relate to each other at the core of our marriage—heart to heart.

Let me go back to my own life. My mind knew the truth (scriptures). God is good. God is love. God never changes. God is compassionate and slow to anger. God is faithful. But in my heart, if I was truly honest and transparent, I really didn't know, believe or think of God in this way. How could I tell?

First, I didn't want to go to Him when I blew it. I was afraid He would be so angry with me and disappointed. When I sinned or was struggling in my walk, I felt God couldn't love me anymore because I felt so horrible or ugly. The bottom line, my heart didn't know—ginosko—the goodness & grace of God and how He loved me, even when I failed.

Then I learned Psalm 51:6. (NASB). *"Behold, You desire truth in the innermost being."* The Hebrew word for innermost being is "touché"(too-chaw'). It means inner regions, hidden recesses, & inward parts.

As I pondered why the Lord would desire truth to dwell in our innermost being, I got the following verse. John 8:32 (ESV)—*"You shall know the truth and the truth shall set you free."*

Then it hit me. The Lord wanted me to know the truth of HIM, and of His character and nature, so that I could be set free—from strongholds of thinking that weren't aligned to who He really was and from the lies of the enemy that I believed.

As I pondered this, I got the following verse. Psalm 139:23-24: *"Search me, O God, and know my heart; Try me and know my anxious thoughts; And see if there be any hurtful way in me, And lead me in the everlasting way."*

So I began to pray for my own heart. I gave God permission to search my heart. And I prayed that the eyes of my heart would be enlightened & that my heart would truly know

God—personally and intimately. I also meditated on these scriptures, asking the Lord to renew my mind so that I would see and perceive things the way He does.

Then God began to do an amazing thing. He gave my heart revelation of His goodness and His unconditional love. The Truth is He loves me, even when I fail. For a child that grew up experiencing conditional love based on my performance, this was truth that set my heart free. This has transformed the way I look at myself, the foundation of my self-esteem, my God confidence, and me. Have I arrived? No. There are moments where I forget this truth and have to go back and remember His goodness, faithfulness, and amazing grace. And thankfully, the Holy Spirit helps to realign my heart and transform my thinking.

What we think about God is crucial. This heart revelation will drive our life and affect our identity in Christ. There's a saying I recently heard. "If you do not see it, you can't become it. Identity must be visualized before it can be realized." *Daniel 11:32 (NASB)—says, "The people who know their God will display strength and take action."*

When we believe that God is for us and not against us, when we believe that He loves us period and that we can approach His throne of grace anytime, at our highest highs or our lowest lows, this will impact our self esteem and our identity in Christ. We are sons and daughters of the most High God. When we truly begin to know this truth in our innermost being, our lives will become transformed.

One of the primary results of experience is to change concepts into heart beliefs. This being so, it is crucial that we experience Jesus through relationship—heart to heart.

I remember the day He began to really speak to my heart about these things.

"Liza, you can boldly enter and draw near to My throne of grace because your confidence is based on the blood I shed on the cross; not your works, not if you're having a great day, or experiencing a terrible one. If you feel victorious in Me one day, and then come to Me in self-confidence, that is pride. If you feel horrible, ugly and plain crabby and avoid coming to Me, then you've missed My grace and have come under condemnation, shame, and doubt/unbelief. This is NOT of Me. You are worthy, because you've been bought with My blood and have become worthy—simply because of My forgiveness and grace. It's nothing about you—but all about Me. That's why you are so beautiful to Me. You're covered with and by My blood."

Hebrews 10:10, 14 (NLT)
"For God's will was for us to be made holy by the sacrifice of the body of Jesus Christ, once for all time. For by that one offering he forever made perfect those who are being made holy."

In February of 2008, while on Oahu at a conference, I had my eyes closed in worship. I was immediately horrified to see a picture of my arms and body covered with blood. "What the heck is this Jesus?" Immediately, I sensed in my spirit that I was covered with His blood. Suddenly, I saw everyone at the conference covered with His blood. Honestly, it was pretty graphic and it shocked me. Then He said, "Let me show you what I see. Suddenly I saw everyone, including me, all dressed in pure white and we shined with His glory. It was only because of the power of His blood and His amazing grace that we were dressed and covered with His glory. We didn't deserve it. We didn't earn it. But because we asked Him for forgiveness and received Him and His Holy Spirit into our hearts and lives, His blood now covered us. And that alone made us worthy and holy. Period!

When our worth is based on self (on what we do for Him & on our performance), we've missed it. If our total worth is based on the truth that we're worthy simply because we've been totally saved, cleaned, & redeemed by His blood shed on the cross (and nothing based on our own self worth), we will experience total grace and thus freedom in walking as sons and daughters of the most high God. We are royalty in His family because we are His children.

6/16/09
Journal entry:

I was waiting on the Lord. He wanted me to come with Him. He had something to show me. As we walked the path, I kept hearing "Look at the trees, look at the trees!" I kept falling asleep. Every time I'd wake up, He was there waiting. "C'mon! Look at the trees!" Finally, I could see these trees covered with fruit. Again, Jesus said, "Look closely. What do you see?" As I looked, I could see birds and other animals looking at the fruit on the trees. They wanted to eat the fruit but they were just waiting in the distance. The fruit remained untouched. Then Jesus asked me, "What color is the fruit?" Suddenly, I saw that all the fruit on the trees were red. Then He said, 'It's red because it's covered with My blood. And because the fruit were covered with My blood, it couldn't be eaten or destroyed by these birds and any other varmints."

As I pondered what the Lord had shown me, I instantly thought of the parable of the seeds. In this story, it was a bird that came and ate all the good seeds that fell on the hard road. In this case, a bird represented the enemy. As I thought about fruit and all that fruit symbolizes and represents in our Christian lives, again I was reminded of this truth:

𝕿here is power in the blood of Jesus.

04/03/08
Journal Entry:

I had a heavy dream this morning. In one part of it, I was half asleep with my eyes closed. I could see a demon with boxing gloves on. I spoke out loud and applied the blood of Jesus to it. And the demon immediately shrunk. I rebuked it in Jesus' name, and then it left. Then another demon appeared. I applied the blood of Jesus to it and it instantly shrunk too. When I woke up, again I was deeply struck by the truth that the blood of Jesus is the most powerful thing in the universe.

09/09/12
Journal Entry:

As I was typing out this final chapter, I heard in the background a line from a movie that my family was watching. It was a Disney cartoon called "The Incredibles." I was hit by the power of God as I heard the mother, Helen Parr, speaking the following words of life to her daughter Violet.

"But things are different now. And doubt is a luxury we can't afford anymore, sweetie. You have more power than you realize. Don't think. And don't worry! If the time comes, you'll know what to do. It's in your blood."

Things are different now. These are the end times and we're living in the last days. Doubt is something we can't afford anymore. You do have more power in you than you realize. His power resides in you. Don't worry! Don't fear! When the time comes, you'll know what to do. His Holy Spirit will guide and empower you. It's in your blood because you are of the bloodline of the King of Kings. And His blood covers you. So rise up into the fullness of the incredible child of God that He created you to be. It's your destiny.

Chapter 7
BE STILL and Rest in Christ

Psalm 46:10(NIV)
"Be still and know that I am God."
In the NASB, it says, "Cease striving (raphah) and know
(yadah) that I am God ('elohiym)."

Cease comes from the Hebrew word "Raphah" which means to relax, to let drop, to let go/forsake, to be quiet. The word "KNOW" comes from the Hebrew word "yada" which refers to know by experience, to recognize, to perceive and see. It is very similar to the Greek word "ginoskos" that we talked about in the previous chapter. GOD in this verse comes from the Hebrew word "elohim." It is the first name of God mentioned in the bible. (Genesis 1:1-2). In the traditional Jewish perspective, Elohim is the name of God as the Creator and Judge of the universe.

Psalm 37:7-9 (ESV)-
"Be still before the LORD and wait patiently for him; fret not
yourself over the one who prospers in his way, over the man
who carries out evil devices. Refrain from anger, and forsake
wrath! Fret not yourself; it tends only to evil. For the evildoers
shall be cut off, but those who wait for the LORD shall inherit
the land."

The Lord makes it very clear that we need to BE STILL! We need to cease striving and to learn how to rest in Him. Part of this comes when we understand what it means to abide in Christ. And practically, this also means that we need to make time and spend time with Jesus.

At this point, let me share another example from my life. In the past, when I heard that I needed to "be still" and spend time with Jesus, I would immediately feel convicted and sometimes condemned that I wasn't spending enough time with my Lord. So as best as I could, in my own strength, I would make a little window of time in my day to open my bible, read a passage in the scripture, try to get something out of it, and then say a quick prayer at the end. But I did this mainly out of guilt and duty. When I was finished, I would then make a mental check off my "list." Basically, I thought I did my Christian duty-what was required of me because I was a follower of Jesus. And in my mind and understanding, I thought I had just spent time with Jesus.

Now I realize the hard truth that I wasn't really being still and spending time with Him. Not really. As followers of Jesus, we each have a personal relationship with Him and one that is suppose to be personal, deep and intimate—heart to heart. In the past, I didn't understand this.

Imagine if in my marriage with Dwight, it all became doing things out of duty. I did the wash for him. I cooked for him. I cleaned the bathroom and bedroom for him. And I did it all because it was the right thing to do. But what if we didn't spend time together, listening to each other, or sharing our hearts, thoughts and experiences together. In reality, we would simply be living in the same house but living totally separate lives. Or imagine that if we did get together, all I did was talk, talk, talk. And I never spent anytime listening to him, hearing how his day went, what he was feeling and thinking, etc. What a lopsided relationship. Either way, I think we'd agree that these aren't great descriptions of what a healthy, intimate marriage relationship would look like. Unfortunately, these 2 examples sadly describe the true state and condition of the types of relationship that many followers have with Jesus. Either we just do things out of "Christian duty" but rarely if ever spend quality time together with Him—living separately and distantly in heart from Him; or we just yak and talk to God but rarely if ever listen to His voice and truly hear what's on His heart.

Many of us are busy. I know. I have 3 kids. And my husband and I help to shepherd a small church. I understand. But time is the currency of this hour. Not money. So how are you spending it? What I've found in my own life is that good sometimes is the greatest enemy of best. Think of all the things you have on your "plate". How many of these things and/ or activities did you honestly ask Jesus about? If we're too busy for God, or doing "good" things for God at the expense of spending time with Him and listening to His heart, we are in dangerous territory. Part of the danger is that we may be investing our time doing good things that He never asked us to do. And tragically, it may be possible that in our busyness of doing good things for God, that we may miss His best and ultimately miss Him. So in this hour, it is crucial that we are all learning to hear and listen to His Voice.

It always fascinates me that when God came to Elijah, He came with a voice as a gentle whisper. 1 Kings 19:11-13 (NIV) states: "The LORD said, "Go out and stand on the mountain in the presence of the LORD, for the LORD is about to pass by." Then a great and powerful wind tore the mountains apart and shattered the rocks before the LORD, but the LORD was not in the wind. After the wind there was an earthquake, but the LORD was not in the earthquake. After the earthquake came a fire, but the LORD was not in the fire. And after the fire came a gentle whisper. When Elijah heard it, he pulled his cloak over his face and went out and stood at the mouth of the cave."

It's a lot easier to hear someone shouting versus someone whispering. When someone is yelling, you can't help but hear his/her voice over the crowd, even if you don't want to listen. But if someone is whispering to us, it takes time and intentionality to focus & to hear what that person is saying. Likewise, it will take us choosing to make the time and to be intentional in listening to His gentle whisper.

3/10/11
Journal Entry:

At a women's bible study, we spent time being still before the Lord. As I waited in stillness before Him, I got the following picture:

I saw a bucket with cleaning materials in it. Every one of the ladies in our group had one. I wasn't sure what it meant. Were we supposed to clean something? Then I saw Jesus. He was using each bucket to clean each person and then cleaning each one as they were still before Him and in His presence. Then Jesus looked at me and humorously said, "It's kind of hard to clean something that is moving." Being still before God is so important.

3/15/11
Journal Entry:

Being prepared for what is to come:
To be still
To live in the grace of God

To be aware of His Presence
To be at rest

When we do not dwell in rest and peace, we will find ourselves reacting to situations. We will react out of our flesh rather than from a place of rest and peace.

———

Finally to end this section on being still and resting in God, I do believe there is a close link between resting and abiding in Christ. In John 15:1-7 (ESV), Jesus said, "*I am the true vine, and my Father is the vinedresser. Every branch in me that does not bear fruit he takes away, and every branch that does bear fruit he prunes, that it may bear more fruit. Already you are clean because of the word that I have spoken to you. Abide in me, and I in you. As the branch cannot bear fruit by itself, unless it abides in the vine, neither can you, unless you abide in me. I am the vine; you are the branches. Whoever abides in me and I in him, he it is that bears much fruit, for apart from me you can do nothing. If anyone does not abide in me he is thrown away like a branch and withers; and the branches are gathered, thrown into the fire, and burned. If you abide in me, and my words abide in you, ask whatever you wish, and it will be done for you.*"

A large part of learning to abide in Christ is learning to rest in our position and place in Christ because of the cross and the blood He shed on the cross. The article below was helpful to me in explaining what it means to abide in Christ.

"Choosing to Abide" by Graham Cooke,
(posted 06/12 by brilliantbookhouse.com)

It is God that has established us in Christ. It is our choice to remain (and rest) where He has so wonderfully placed us. Choosing to "Abide in First Love" literally means occupying the space between the Father and the Son and learning to abide in love. Abiding is concerned with maintaining a place of intimate connection with the Father and the Son, aided by the loving support and power of the Holy Spirit. "Keep yourself in the love of God." (Jude 1:21)

When we do not consciously abide, we suffer a disconnect in our fellowship with God. We must pay attention to the place of where we live from in the Spirit and stay! It is vital that we understand the difference between relationship and fellowship, or we cannot walk with God in consistent passion and power. The true place of abiding is between these two points.

Relationship means we are of the same blood. It is based on the unconditional love that the Father has for the Son. This is the paramount reason why God put us into Christ. Now we are partakers of His holiness. Relationship is forever possible because of the sacrifice of Jesus. In relationship we stand in His righteousness and are given grace to conform to God's image. It's all about placement. God takes care of the relationship; we take care of the fellowship. Abiding is the practice of staying in fellowship. We don't do anything to get into the Presence of God (salvation is a gift), but we must do everything to stay there. Fellowship is about developing, with the help of the Holy Spirit, the present-to-the-moment lifestyle of abiding . . . staying where we have been placed. The Father has put us into relationship with Jesus and He will not take us out of this placement. The work of the Holy Spirit is to enable us to stay in that place and enjoy the benefits of consistent fellowship.

The story of the prodigal in Luke 15 is a real testament to the issue of relationship and fellowship. The wasteful son thought he could return home and be accepted as a servant. He thought his sins had damaged his relationship with his father. The Father ran to the son because He had always carried the burden of fellowship. The Father celebrated because the fellowship had been restored. The relationship was never in doubt! Both sons did not understand that relationship and fellowship were very different.

God abides in relationship. We abide in fellowship. He maintains the relationship. We maintain the fellowship. Jesus stands before the Father as the Giver of relationship. The Holy Spirit works in our lives as the Empowerer of fellowship.

If you have resolved the issues of first love; relationship and fellowship and identity through intimacy, (this) will be a huge step forward in your development. There are huge breakthroughs to be received and processed into ongoing experiences as these messages begin to penetrate the layers of spiritual blindness that is the lasting legacy of a religious spirit. When the keys of the Kingdom are present then the truth that sets us free will open every prison door. It is for freedom that Christ has set us free. The love of God for us is the gateway to that freedom.

Chapter 8
Kingdom Perspective: His Sheep Hear His Voice

I was 13 years old when I first received Jesus into my life. I remember being so excited about my new life in Christ. As I was discipled in my home church, I was taught that I needed to read the bible every day, pray every day, memorize scripture, and go to church every Sunday. I am deeply grateful that I learned a lot of biblical knowledge. But as I went through high school & college, and I faced life decisions, like where should I apply for college & whom should I marry, I found that I struggled to know God's will for my life. And as I began to yearn and hunger to know His heart and will for my life, I began to realize that although I had a personal relationship with Jesus, I still really didn't know Him or have a deep, intimate friendship with Him; nor did I understand what it meant to "hear" God's voice. So I began to ask questions.

If Jesus was suppose to be my best friend, how come I didn't deeply know Him including recognizing how He spoke & communicated His heart to me. If I did have a personal relationship with Jesus, how come the depth and quality of my relationship with Him seemed distant and seemed dry & more like I was doing religious activity versus experiencing true friendship with Jesus?

As my journey with Jesus continued, I began to meet believers who demonstrated deep authentic humility, love, grace and the fruit of the Spirit in their lives. They also possessed such a genuine, deep relationship with Jesus that included flowing in the gifts of the Spirit that I found so attractive and beautiful. And as I watched their personal lives, I began to see a common thread; they made it a top priority to spend quality time alone with Jesus. I was intrigued.

Looking back at my own personal quiet times, I honestly confess that a large part of it was simply doing religious activity versus intimately connecting with Jesus, my Lord and the love of my life.

Sadly, my quiet time looked like a rigid to do list.

1. Read a scripture. Check.
2. Read a personal story that came with my devotions. Check.
3. Answer the personal question at the end of the reading. Check.
4. Pray my prayer list at the end. Check.
5. List done. Check.
6. Quiet time with Jesus—done! Check.
7. Move on to the next part of my day . . .

After I was done, I felt pretty good about myself. I'd pat myself on the back and felt I was a "strong" Christian because I read my bible and I prayed which was the right thing to do. I also felt relieved that I did my Christian duty to "spend time" with Jesus. Sadly, I honestly didn't remember most of what I read or prayed about, even 15-30 minutes later. Can anyone relate? At this point, I do want to clarify that I am not putting down devotional guides. What I am trying to point out was the state of my heart and the perspective I had about what praying and spending time with Jesus was all about.

I also remember struggling to pray even 5 minutes while going through my checklist of prayer requests. That was what I thought prayer time with Jesus looked like—just tell Him my list of prayer requests and what I wanted Him to do. Prayer lists are good things. I still use them. But with the perspective I had at that time, I was missing the point. After a few minutes, I was usually done with my list and then I didn't know what to pray next. So my prayer times were usually very short and also one sided. I did all the talking and spent very little time, if any, listening to Him.

A part of not knowing or understanding this difference came simply from ignorance. It was also what I was taught and modeled by most of the Christians around me at that time. This was largely because this was all they understood what it meant to be a Christian. They lovingly shared what they knew with me. And I am grateful for all their love, their prayers and their time that they invested in me. But what many of us didn't understand or experience on a much deeper level was that it was about relationship, not a religious to do list.

One of my favorite authors is Francis Frangipane. He says, "Religion without love is an abomination to God. The Church needs to learn that God desires love and compassion, not merely an adherence to ritual and sacrifice."

For me, there was a point in my own personal walk with God when I sadly realized that a lot of my relationship with Jesus was about adhering to ritual and sacrifice, not about intimacy and relationship with Him. And I felt dry like a scorched desert in my soul. But desperation is a good thing. I cried out to Jesus. "There's got to be more than this Lord! I need You! If I don't encounter You, I will wither up, spiritually. I don't want religion. I want the real and the authentic! But I don't know how to hear Your voice Lord at least the way I see others hear You. I need help so please help me Jesus!

Breakthrough in me! Meet me! You promised that if I draw near to You, You will draw near to me." Yes, I was hungry and desperate for more of Him.

And God is so faithful. He proved to me again that *"Blessed are those who hunger and thirst for righteousness, for they shall be satisfied."* Matthew 5:6 (ESV). *"Blessed are the poor in spirit, for theirs is the kingdom of heaven."* Matthew 5:3 (ESV). I was hungry and desperate spiritually and I was definitely poor in spirit. The awesome news was that He satisfied me and met me where I was. Today I am experiencing a much deeper level and intimate relationship with Jesus and I am learning more and more what it is to know that the Kingdom of Heaven is my inheritance as His child.

It is a good thing to be honest and transparent with God. I have found that true humility before Him deeply touches His heart of mercy and compassion for us. Psalm 34:18 states, *"The Lord is near to the brokenhearted and saves the crushed in spirit."* In the Amplified Bible, it says, *"The Lord is close to those who are of a broken heart and saves such as are crushed with sorrow for sin and are humbly and thoroughly penitent."* *What good news! What awesome truth and amazing grace!*

What I have learned and experienced is that God loves to communicate with us. It's His nature. He created humans out of His desire to have deep, intimate relationship with them. And He made each of us unique so the way He "speaks" to each of us is personal and creatively unique. Sometimes His Voice is heard through a dream or vision. Sometimes His Voice is heard through Scripture. Sometimes His Voice is heard through the wisdom shared through another follower of Jesus. Sometimes His Voice is heard powerfully through an anointed song. Sometimes His voice is heard through a beautiful sunset or even a stranger that He allows our paths to cross with. If God chose a donkey to speak to Balaam, He can choose whatever He wishes to be His mouthpiece to communicate to us. The question is, "Are we hearing Him?" And more so, "Are we listening?"

In John 10:2-5 (ESV), it says, *"But he who enters by the door is the shepherd of the sheep. To him the gatekeeper opens. The sheep hear his voice, and he calls his own sheep by name and leads them out. When he has brought out all his own, he goes before them, and the sheep follow him, for they know his voice. A stranger they will not follow, but they will flee from him, for they do not know the voice of strangers."*

The good news is that all of us who are followers of Jesus are wired by the power of the Holy Spirit to hear our Lord's voice. That's what the Word of God says. Looking back, I now see that as a new believer in the Lord, I was like a lamb that needed help in learning how to recognize my Lord's voice. So He sent mature believers to help model that to me. I needed to grow and mature in my own relationship with my Lord so that as a sheep, a mature believer (independent of human aging), I would know and recognize my Lord's "voice." Ultimately, this meant that I needed to make it a priority to make time to "be still and know" Him by spending time listening.

As I was humbled to realize that I didn't know how to recognize my Lord's voice for myself, I remember praying and asking the Holy Spirit to please teach me how to hear His voice so that I could follow Him. And God is so faithful. He answered my simple prayer. First, He put mature, spirit filled believers into my life. Then He began to use them to model and to help me grow in learning to discern and "hear" the Lord's voice for myself. He led me to awesome teachers and their powerful teaching books & DVDs, like Donna Jordan, an instructor from YWAM, who taught on listening to God.

At this point, may I ask you an honest question. Do you know and recognize our Lord's voice? Or is this something that you need to mature and grow in? It's okay if at this point you don't. Jesus always communicates truth with grace and love. If the truth is that you still don't know how to recognize our Lord's voice, there is absolutely no condemnation in Christ. He loves you. And He deeply desires you and I to grow deeply and intimately in our personal relationships with Him. He wants us to recognize and hear His voice.

In John 8:32 (ESV), it states, *"You shall know the truth and the truth shall set you free."* Just be truthful and honest with God. And He will set you free.

If you honestly desire to know and recognize His voice, **please pray this simple prayer** with me. *"Lord help me to hear and recognize Your Voice. In Your Name, amen."*

God is faithful and good. He answered "YES!" to my simple prayer, And I know He will answer yours, all because it is in His nature to do so. He is good. And He is love. Jesus is so creative. He's the most creative being in the universe. And He's wired and made us so different and unique. The way He chooses to speak to me isn't necessarily the same way He may choose to speak to you and to others.

For some of His children, He allows them to "hear" and recognize His voice as He communicates through vivid dreams and/or visions. He allows others to see the spirit world as clearly as the physical world to help the body of Christ discern His will. To others, He speaks through a particular scripture or passage. To others, He speaks and communicates through nature. To others, He uses an audible voice. Some people get very vivid pictures and visions. The key is not to compare yourself with others but to spend time with Jesus daily. And as you do, you will grow by the power of His Holy Spirit, to recognize the way He talks and communicates with you and you will hear His voice.

It is also wisdom and love to recognize that the way He speaks to each of us may be different and because of that, we shouldn't force and think that everyone has to hear God the way we do. For me, this has been a lesson of wisdom and love that I am learning. We all need to simply stop comparing ourselves to others and to stop forcing others to only experience and hear God the way that each of us does.

I have found that if I use others as my mode of comparison and standard, I would get really puffed up with pride or become super discouraged. I have also found that if I leave out love and wisdom, I can become quite legalistic and religious about certain things, even with something as beautiful as learning to hear His voice. He knows each of us intimately. He knows that if He speaks in just one way, many of us would miss out because we're wired differently. So many times, He chooses to communicate to each of us on a one to one basis. What an awesome, personal Lord we serve and follow. Ultimately, we are His sheep who hear His voice because He is our shepherd. His blood that He shed on the cross at Calvary covers us and makes us His sheep. There's no room for pride or discouragement in His Kingdom. He loves each of us and He promises that we, as His sheep, will hear and recognize His voice.

Chapter 9
Kingdom Perspective: God loves to share His secrets with His friends.

During one of my times of waiting on Him, I heard Him say, "I have so many secrets to tell My children if only they would stop & listen." Psalm 25:14 (ESV) again states, *"The friendship of the Lord is for those who fear him."* Interestingly, the NASB says, *"The secret of the Lord is for those who fear him."* If you look up the word "friendship/secret" from this verse in Strong's Concordance, the Hebrew word for this is "cowd" (sode). It means "council, counsel, assembly, secret counsel, & intimacy (with God)." Jesus wants all of His children to have a deep, intimate relationship with Him and He wants to share the things on His heart with them.

Oswald Chambers was an awesome, inspired writer. Utmost.org posted the following article written by him as their word for June 3rd, 2012. (www. http://utmost.org/the-secret-of-the-lord/My Utmost for His Highest) Here is the first half of that post.

The secret of the Lord is with those who fear Him . . .
—Psalm 25:14

What is the sign of a friend? Is it that he tells you his secret sorrows? No, it is that he tells you his secret joys. Many people will confide their secret sorrows to you, but the final mark of intimacy is when they share their secret joys with you. Have we ever let God tell us any of His joys? Or are we continually telling God our secrets, leaving Him no time to talk to us? At the beginning of our Christian life we are full of requests to God. But then we find that God wants to get us into an intimate relationship with Himself— to get us in touch with His purposes. Are we so intimately united to Jesus Christ's idea of prayer— "Your will be done" (Matthew 6:10)— that we catch the secrets of God? What makes God so dear to us is not so much His big blessings to us, but the tiny things, because they show His amazing intimacy with us— He knows every detail of each of our individual lives.

Isn't that beautiful? Osward Chambers shares that the final mark of intimacy in a friendship is when they share their secret joys with you. Have we ever let God tell us any of His joys? I deeply desire to be a friend of God.

As I've spent time with the Lord, I've filled a lot of journals with the things He's shared with me. As I've gone through them, I've found some journal entries that didn't really fit in any other chapter. Some entries I have not shared because I was told not to. But the following entries I felt needed to be included in this book. For me, these are special because some contain personal promises and some really showed me His heart. I earnestly pray that whatever He desires to impart and reveal through these entries would be accomplished.

I also pray that as you read this section, your desire to spend time with Him in the secret place of intimacy would deepen and grow. And I know He will speak and show Himself to you because of who He is. His nature is one of pure goodness, faithfulness, kindness, gentleness & love.

7/27/06
Journal Entry:

Tonight, you gave me more verses. Deut. 30:6, 9, 10

"And the Lord will circumcise your heart and the heart of your offspring, so that you will love the LORD your God with all your heart and with all your soul, that you may live. The LORD your God will make you abundantly prosperous in all the work of your hand. For the LORD will again take delight in prospering you **when you obey the voice of the LORD your God**, *to keep His commandments and His statutes that are written in this book of the law,* **when you turn to the LORD your God will all your heart and with all your soul."**

Yes Lord. It is vital to hear Your voice and follow through with obedience with all of my heart and soul. Thank you Jesus! As I pondered these things, I saw a white cloud appear as Your presence filled our bedroom right by the ceiling. It looked like a haze and there was light right above me. I really sensed the presence of Jesus. He was here even though I couldn't physically see Him.

11/26/06
Journal Entry:

What an amazing experience! It was 3:30 a.m. I was so tired from working on our children's ministry things. I got on my knees. As soon as I did that, I felt so much better. You filled me instantly with peace and joy. Then I lay down to sleep. At first I got stuck in that dimension I hate where I couldn't move with my eyes closed, half asleep. I cried to you. Then I woke up still with my eyes shut when suddenly, you gave me my first real tangible vision. We were dancing. I was spinning and spinning. I was dressed like a princess ballet dancer. My hair was swept up in a bun. And I had something like a white crown or hairpiece on my head. The guy I was dancing with was you-Jesus! You were dressed so debonair and handsome, like a prince. At that point, I should have kept my eyes shut, but I opened them. As I looked up, I was shocked to see the outline of a female angel right above me and she was shaking her head "No." I apologized and said, "I'm sorry" and I quickly closed my eyes. I felt images & light swirling around but my mind was racing and I couldn't see or focus on anything. I then told Jesus, "I'm sorry. Please give me revelation of all that it means." But I felt SO LOVED!

12/3/06
Journal Entry:

This morning, as I was waiting upon You, I saw tons of open blue sky in the ceiling above me. So I asked Jesus, "Please show me Your heavenly kingdom." Suddenly, I could see myself sitting on a white horse that was standing still. In the distance, I saw a huge, giant warrior in a roman type gladiator outfit standing on a hill, surrounded by white horses with smaller regular sized warriors sitting on them. There were also regular size warriors standing in battle readiness with them. I asked Jesus, "Who's that?" He said, "That's Me." (So matter of fact) Then I saw Jesus as the huge giant warrior lift His hand up and point forward (like the signal to charge). Later, as I sat up in my bed, you spoke to my heart—"The Final Battle has begun."

2/8/07
Journal Entry:

Sitting in bed, waiting on the Lord, I saw a vision. I was moving down a tunnel really fast, like in a speeding car. I then realized that this tunnel was really a hallway with doors. Each door had writing on it. Then the vision slowed down and a door in the distance opened out. I couldn't see what was written on the door. Then the door opened and the vision continued through the door. As it did, it entered into another hallway with doors. And at the end of this 2nd hallway, 2 doors were opened inwards like an entryway. The vision continued by going through these 2 doors and then the vision ended.

I asked the Lord what the writing was on the doors. What I got was that the writings on the doors were people's names. Each door had a name written on it. Then I got 2 Chronicles 16:9 (NIV). *"For the eyes of the Lord range throughout the earth to strengthen those whose hearts are fully committed to him."* The vision I had was really about Jesus and His passion for us. Each door represented a person's life. The 2nd double doors represented the doors to a person's heart. Jesus was the one running down these hallways, passionately searching for any open doors of lives and hearts that were open to Him. I will never forget what His heart felt like as He was passionately searching for open hearts. He really loves us and desires intimacy with His children.

4/24/07
Journal Entry:

I had a very heavy vision this morning as I woke up and was lying in bed. I saw outer space. In the vision, I was whizzing through space and found myself traveling through a tunnel. It felt like a roller coaster joy ride until I looked in the distance and was horrified as I realized this tunnel was headed for a black hole in outer space. I saw white spots traveling through this tunnel towards the black hole. What I sensed was that this was a tunnel filled with lost souls headed for hell. I felt so sad. There were thousands upon thousands of souls in that tunnel. And I remember seeing a close up of the tunnel right at the end, seeing an outline of a white human shape falling into the dark hole. It was tragic. And then Matthew 7:13 (NLT) came to mind. *"You can enter God's Kingdom only through the narrow gate. The highway to hell is broad, and its gate is wide for the many who choose that way."*

11/11/07
Journal Entry:

Rise up as history makers. Spending time with Jesus is the only tool to sustain His fire in your life. We need to seek His face. Don't seek the things God can do. Seek His face first. We owe the world an encounter with Jesus. We need renewed minds that aren't intimidated by our situations. Faith is spelled "RISK."

1/21/08
Journal entry:
Jesus spoke the following to my heart in
the quietness of the night.

"There are books to be written by you, my precious child. Be faithful and choose to love and embrace the things you are walking through. Do you remember that prophetic picture your friend gave you? He saw you walking through open fields and a path formed behind you. And as you walked, you dropped gems along the path. Liza, I've designed you to be a trailblazer. And yes, you will drop gemstones along the path to help others that follow. Close your eyes, I have something to show you."

As I closed my eyes, I saw a beautiful tree made with silver bark and golden apples. There were baskets underneath the tree on the ground. Jesus was picking fruit. He was wearing white. Then I saw a woman reading a book. Fruit like a pear came out of the book as she read it, and she ate the pear. Then she became a beautiful tree that produced the same golden fruit. Right after that, Jesus spoke. "Your books will be food for others to eat, grow and flourish."

Jesus, I receive Your words. I choose to believe. Help me Holy Spirit to hear You clearly and to obey You in all things for the sake of Your kingdom and for Your glory.

2/4/08
Journal Entry:

The kids and I spent time being still, listening, & soaking in the presence of Jesus. Immediately I could see myself in the middle of a beautiful field of white daisies. I was wearing a white dress. Up ahead was a hill with a beautiful big tree on top of it. Jesus was standing under it waiting for me. Then I was with Him, sitting on a swing under the tree and He was laughing, smiling and pushing me on the swing. As I went higher, I then heard Him say to me, "It's time to fly child, so fly." I was a bit scared, so I held on to the ropes of the swings tighter. Then, after taking a breath, I leapt off the swing . . . and I was flying!!! Then Jesus was in the air flying with me.

Then I saw a table stacked with books; books that I needed to write. Then Jesus spoke to me. "It's time to write The Kingdom Perspective."

Then my 3 kids needed my attention and I had to go . . .

3/2/08
Journal Entry:

Jesus had me open up my hand. He then placed a journal into it. Jesus then said, "Open it up Liza." So I did. I opened the journal up to the first page. It was blank. Then in my right hand, He placed a gold pen. "Now start writing." I sensed I was supposed to write the title of the book on it. So I wrote, "The Kingdom Perspective." Instantly, the book was filled with pages and pages of writing. I was astonished and happily surprised. Thank you Jesus!

05/28/08
Journal Entry:

I saw Jesus extend His hand out. "Come with me," He said. So I took His hand and followed. We then sat by a flow of hot red lava. Jesus was wearing white with a red sash. Then He spoke.

"This fire that is being spread all over the world is different. Its intensity in a person is aligned with each individual's surrender and yieldedness. For those that allow Me, in an instant, the fire of this anointing is like the lava, hot and intense, and it will bring impurities to the surface. This lava, this fire, is fluid like water. It will flow down the path of least resistance. When there is pride in a person's heart, it's like a pile of rocks lifted up. The lava goes around it and that part remains unchanged. The fire will only refine the part that is yielded and surrendered. It is difficult for those who have soared previously to yield and surrender."

09/02/08
Journal Entry:

A few weeks ago, as I was soaking in Your presence, I heard You say, "You are Terra Nova." I had no clue what that meant. I finally looked it up today. One of the definitions for Terra Nova was "new land."

"Jesus, speak Your heart to me." I prayed. Then He spoke to my heart.

"Fear, insecurities, rejection . . . These are the things I am bringing to the surface during this time. Don't feel sorry for these young ones. It is My will that they are walking through this difficult time because of their future destinies. Trust Me. Trust Me to fulfill My purposes in each of them. Don't worry. I am faithful.

My yoke is easy and My burden is light. I know that it doesn't feel like this right now. But I have allowed this during this time. I will carry you both and your children. I will carry it for this is My burden alone to bear. Just be you—in Me.

You are Terra Nova. I've made you into the new. Don't go back to being the old. New land . . . new wineskins."

I love You Jesus! You are worth everything and I surrender everything to You. Jesus, lead us. I pray You will show us Your heart. We need to hear Your heart.

01/09
Journal Entry:

I saw Jesus walking through a garden. And I saw flowers, tons of them in all different colors, shapes, & sizes. But they were all beautiful. As He walked through the garden, He began to pick flowers, all for His pleasure. As He picked a bunch of flowers, He gently removed thorns from them. Then He picked other flowers and gently brushed off dirt/pebbles. He picked more flowers and then trimmed off leaves. As He did all of this, He smelled each flower with delight as He breathed in each one's unique fragrance. He enjoyed each flower's individual beauty. And He was pleased.

This was such a beautiful picture that the Lord gave to me. But honestly, sometimes I had a hard time believing this truth that I was a beautiful flower to Him, even with my thorns, dirt and extra foliage. I struggled with my identity and who I was in Christ. I knew this truth in my head, but sometimes I had a hard time believing this in my heart. I remember moments where I didn't feel beautiful like the flowers I saw Jesus pick. I would see my weaknesses and shortcomings, (and sometimes even sin) and then I couldn't believe that I was still a beautiful flower to Him. I would even feel very ugly and unwanted.

As I examined those times when I would feel this way, I realized that those moments happened when my eyes focused on myself and not on Jesus. I had forgotten who I was in Christ and that His blood covered me. I wouldn't come to Him because I felt shame.

The truth is we all don't deserve His love, but He freely gives it to us anyway. The devil is called the father of lies. Yes, he's a roaring lion and has some power, but for us who are believers and followers of Jesus, he is only as powerful as we believe his lies in our individual lives. It is a lie to believe that we are junk. We're not. The truth is we are created in the image of God.

2 Corinthians 5:17 (NLT)
"This means that anyone who belongs to Christ has become
a new person. The old life is gone; a new life has begun!"
We're new creatures in Christ!

When the truth of who God is, (His divine true nature, His goodness, His amazing grace, His love and mercy for us) is received in our hearts and becomes "known" deeply and intimately in our innermost being, then we will be made truly free. Remember <u>John 8:32 (NASB)</u>? When we **know** the truth of who God really is and His great love for us through the cross, this truth will set us free.

Joshua 24:15 (ESV) states: "*Choose this day whom you will serve.*" Perhaps, at least for me, it's more vital to ask myself, "Choose this day who I will believe." So what and who are you going to choose to believe this day? You are worthy because of the blood of Jesus. Your relationship with Him is from the covenant He made between Himself as the Father and as the Son. It can never be broken. You are His child and are deeply loved. Like the picture He gave me of the garden and flowers, we are all beautiful flowers to Him and He loves our unique colors, fragrances, shapes, etc.

01/23/09
Journal Entry:

I saw a white table decorated (like having tea). Jesus had me sit with Him casually. There was an opening (window) next to the table. As I gazed out the window, I was shocked! I saw what looked like a swirl of chaos outside: gray, dark, and ominous. Yet inside it was really calm and peaceful. The chaos outside couldn't touch us. Then Jesus grew really big (or the swirl got really small). Jesus held out His hand in front of me. And in the center of his palm was the swirl of chaos. He was in total control. And in comparison to Him, the chaos was almost nothing.

My prayer:
"Lord, help me keep my eyes on You."

2/3/09
Journal Entry:
This morning, I was waiting on Jesus. I felt really out of it yesterday and today. Then I saw Jesus' feet first. Then He came over to me and lifted a heavy burden off of me. I saw that it was people's expectations of me. I literally felt lighter and lighter, like I was going to float. And this was all because Jesus removed my heavy burdens. I then saw a beautiful stream. There was a wonderful grassy spot that He took me to.

Psalm 23:2-4 (ESV)
"He makes me lie down in green pastures. He leads me beside still waters. He restores my soul. He leads me in paths of righteousness for his name's sake."

Psalm 16:11 (ESV)
"You make known to me the path of life; in your presence there is fullness of joy;
at your right hand are pleasures forevermore."

02/06/09
Journal Entry:
This is what I heard as I waited on the Lord.

"Sound affects the atmosphere. There's energy and power in sound. Let sound resonate in and through you. Don't limit Me because of what you see in the natural . . . trust Me. Believe . . . have faith. There are colors in heaven, but there also are sounds in heaven." Then I could see myself with arms stretched out with music notes floating all around me.

02/22/09
Journal Entry:
As I waited on the Lord, I got the following picture:

I saw Aimee Semple McPherson approaching me. Once she came up to me, she began to speak.

"Liza, I made a lot of mistakes. Although my anointing was great, I had wounds. I did not have a system of accountability over and around me. And thus I made a lot of mistakes. God is truly a God of Grace. As you can see, in spite of my personal choices and mistakes, I am still a general in heaven. God knows my heart. Take what is good from my life and throw out the bad. Social justice was huge for me. Revival was my burning passion and healing was a tool. Although my personal life was in shambles at the time, God gave me a heart of love that transcended age, race, color. By God's grace, I had a heart that loved people.

You are blessed Liza. You have a humble, mighty man of God who covers you well. Stay under his covering and you will flourish. You aren't meant to be me. Your ministry will not look like mine. Neither are you supposed to act or imitate me. Rise up daughter. Do not be afraid. Keep your eyes on Jesus at all times and remain steadfast and accountable to those the Lord has placed over you. You are truly blessed. Be faithful dear sister in the Lord and run the race well. If you do, you will not face the bitter loving judgment that I had when I stood before the throne of our heavenly father. Rise up. It is time to prepare the way of our Lord on Earth. I am praying and interceding for you, as are the others, including your son Koby. Never put me on a pedestal. And never put yourself on a pedestal. That was my mistake. We are sisters in Christ first. Never forget that.

10/7/09
Journal Entry:

I felt compelled to pray and press in for the past 3 days. This morning, I immediately sat down and waited. Jesus was calling. I felt horribly dirty and unworthy as I saw my shortcomings and fears. Jesus knew what I was thinking and feeling. So He spoke. "My mercies are new every morning Liza. Receive my love and grace." So I did.

Jesus appeared to me dressed as a Lord, with a royal cape, mostly all white with a bit of blue. Jesus said He was dressed this way to help me recognize His role at that moment. Jesus then asked me a question. "Who are you Liza?" Immediately I knew He was also referring to the role He had chosen for me before time began. "I chose you before time to be in this place and role. Walk into your destiny! You have been given much. Therefore much is required."

Then Jesus talked to me about this book. "How long do I have Lord?" I asked. Then I saw Him point 1 finger in the air. "What? One year? (No.) One month? (No.)" Then He said, "One season." I had no clue what He meant by that so I asked, "How long is that?" "3 months", he said. YIKES!!!! As I did the math in my head, I realized I had until the end of December to finish the first draft. "Lord, I need help!" He did answer and showed me a few more things. This really encouraged my heart.

11/13/09
Journal Entry:

This morning, You came! Oh how I love Your presence! Then I heard "47." I didn't know what that meant. Then Jesus said, "You have 47 days left to complete the book (the first draft)." YIKES!!!! I took out my calendar. I counted 47 days from today and found it was right to the end of this year. I was feeling a bit stressed as I realized I had such little time left to finish this manuscript. So I prayed. "Jesus, help me to be faithful and to write!" All of a sudden, I could see myself writing and as I did, I saw loaves and loaves of bread. Jesus then spoke and said that this was going to be a source of bread to feed those that would read this book. What a humbling thought!

11/27/09
Journal Entry:

This morning as I was waiting on the Lord, immediately I saw an open heaven over me. Then I got a picture of a person reading The Kingdom Perspective, and as the different chapters were covered, gems of truth came out of the book as gifts to this person. (Thank you for encouraging my heart Jesus! I am grateful.)

12/23/09
Journal Entry:

It's about 3 am. I waited on the Lord in silence. This is what I heard. "You must know your purpose in order to walk forward into your destiny."

01/25/10
Journal Entry:

I could see Jesus walking. "Come follow Me." In front of Him was a huge obstacle looking path. It looked like a basic training obstacle course for the military. I stood there looking at what lay ahead and all I could think of was "Whew!!" Jesus could tell I was a bit overwhelmed by what lay ahead. Then He gently said, "Look behind you." I turned around and saw a HUGE obstacle course behind me. This represented all the difficult trials and obstacles that He had already helped me to go through in my life. I was reminded of my journey and thought about my life and struggles as a single person, through the death of my first born son, the hard and difficult journey of helping my husband shepherd our Elevate church family, and so on. And through it all, Jesus had always been there for me and was so faithful. As I looked forward, with Jesus next to me, I realized the path in front didn't seem so overwhelming and difficult.

Personal Reflection & Conviction:

I believe the Lord desires to impart spiritual gems of truth of His Kingdom to those that read this book with an open teachable child-like heart. This has nothing to do with me, but everything to do with Him & the power of His Holy Spirit. In Mark 10:15 (ESV), Jesus said, *"Truly, I say to you, whoever does not receive the kingdom of God like a child shall not enter it."*

The older I get and the more I experience God, the more I realize how important it is to have child-like faith. If the Lord has stirred your heart while you've read this chapter and you want to experience more of HIM and want to receive all that

He desires to spiritually impart through this book, **please pray with me.**

"Jesus, I want more of You. I want to experience deep, authentic friendship with You. I desire more of Your presence. Please help me to have a supernatural increase of child-like faith. Release Your spirit of wisdom and revelation and open the eyes of my heart to truly see so that I can know You deeply and intimately. (Ephesians 1:17-20) Please keep my heart soft and pliable in Your hands. Having a teachable heart marks true humility. So please keep me humble and teachable before Your throne. Open my eyes to see things as You see them. Fill me with Your love. Impart to me Your Kingdom Perspective on Earth. Prepare me so that I can help prepare the way of the Lord.
I love You Jesus.

Only by Your grace, only by Your blood, only for Your glory!
In Jesus name, amen."

Chapter 10
Kingdom Perspective:
The Favor and Pleasure of God

* The Favor of God

1/25/09
Journal Entry:

Out of obedience to Jesus, I took time today to focus on writing this book. I felt a nudge/desire to go to Starbucks. When I got there and stood in line, I was greeted by the sound of my name. "Oh Liza! Hi!" It was a wonderful older woman of God that Dwight and I knew. As I chatted, I was surprised with delight when she paid for her drink and then said, "And I'm paying for her too. Liza, go get whatever you want. And get a dessert too." I wasn't planning to get anything to eat, mainly because those things are so expensive and simply extravagant. And I felt God smile. This was from Him.

As I picked up my drink, I was stunned when she then bought me a Starbucks gift card and lovingly and generously said "Liza, you come back on your own, and enjoy yourself on us." My eyes got a bit teary as I felt again the favor and extravagance of our God who just wanted to bless me today through this woman.

01/29/09
Journal Entry:

At 3 a.m., the Lord woke me up. As I looked, I saw a key. It looked like a master key (a type of skeleton key) and I saw the word "FAVOR" written on it. He then gave it to me. As I held it in my hand, it became long, huge and continued to grow.

Later, as I pondered about this key of favor that I saw, I really felt impressed to do a short, personal study on favor. Here are a few things that I found and learned.

Psalm 84:11(ESV)
"For the LORD God is a sun and shield; the LORD bestows favor and honor. No good thing does he withhold from those who walk uprightly. O LORD of hosts, blessed is the one who trusts in you!"

*Lesson: The LORD is the one who bestows favor and honor.

Genesis 6:8 (ESV)
"But Noah found favor in the eyes of the LORD."

*Lesson: Favor is found in the eyes of the LORD.

Genesis 39:21 (NASB)
"But the LORD was with Joseph and extended kindness to him, and gave him favor in the sight of the chief jailer."

*Lesson: The Lord was WITH Joseph and the Lord gave him favor.

Exodus 33:17 (NASB)
"The LORD said to Moses, "I will also do this thing of which you have spoken; for you have found favor in My sight and I have known you by name."

*Lesson: <u>Favor is linked with relationship with God. The Lord knew Moses by name.</u>

1 Samuel 2:26 (NASB)
"Now the boy Samuel was growing in stature and in favor both with the LORD and with men."

*Lesson: <u>Favor is something that we can grow in.</u>

Luke 2:52 (NLT)
"Jesus grew in wisdom and in stature and in favor with God and all the people."

Even Jesus as a child grew in favor with God and all people.

Ps 5:12 (NASB)
"For it is You who blesses the righteous man, O LORD, You surround him with favor as with a shield."

*Lesson: <u>God's favor surrounds us like a shield.</u>

Psalm 119:58 (NASB)
"I sought Your favor with all my heart; Be gracious to me according to Your word."

In this verse, favor comes from the Hebrew word "paniym" (paw-neem'). This word means the face and presence of

God. This was written by King David, a man after God's own heart. David sought the favor of God. He was seeking His face and His presence. If we were to replace the word favor in this verse with it's Hebrew meaning, it would read, "I sought Your face and presence with all my heart; Be gracious to me according to Your word".

*Lesson: <u>Seeking God's favor means seeking after His face and His presence.</u>

One of my heroes of the bible who definitely had the favor of God upon her life was Esther. Here are some personal thoughts I had when I studied her life.

Esther 2:7-9 (ESV)
" . . . Hadassah, that is Esther, the daughter of his uncle, for she had neither father nor mother. The young woman had a beautiful figure and was lovely to look at, and when her father and her mother died, Mordecai took her as his own daughter. So when the king's order and his edict were proclaimed, and when many young women were gathered in Susa the citadel in custody of Hegai, Esther also was taken into the king's palace and put in custody of Hegai, who had charge of the women. And the young woman pleased him and won his favor."

Here we see that Esther had pleased and won the favor of this eunuch Hegai. How? Why? Was it simply her physical beauty? I don't think so. Probably most of the young women chosen for the king were the most physically attractive and beautiful in the land.

Then in Esther 2:10 (ESV), we begin to see a clue. *"Esther had not made known her people or kindred, for Mordecai had commander her not to make it known."* And then in Esther 2: 15-17 (ESV), we see another one. *"When the turn came for Esther, the daughter of Abihail the uncle of Mordecai, who had taken her as his own daughter to go in to the king, she asked for nothing except what Hegai the king's eunuch, who had charge of the women, advised. Now Esther was winning favor in the eyes of all who saw her. And when Esther was taken to King Ahasuerus into his royal palace in the tenth month, which is the month of Tebeth, in the seventh year of his reign, the king loved Esther more than all the women, and she won grace and favor in his sight more than all the virgins, so that he set the royal crown on her head and made her queen instead of Vasti."*

So what did I learn from Esther? I believe part of the reason she won such grace and favor in the eyes of all those around her was because she had such a humble heart of obedience. Esther obeyed Mordecai's command not to make known her ethnicity. And when Esther's turn came up to go into the king, she chose to seek the counsel of Haggai and asked for nothing except what he advised. I also believe Esther's favor came partly as a result of seeking wise counsel and being humble enough to receive it. And part of it simply was the sovereignty of God. She was chosen to walk into this role to save her people. And God's grace and favor was upon her to help her fulfill her destiny & purpose.

Proverbs 22:1—(NAS)
"A good name is to be more desired than great wealth, Favor is better than silver and gold."

I love jewelry made out of real gold or sterling silver. Yet the bible says that <u>God's favor is better than silver and gold</u>

and that a good name (good reputation) should be more desired than seeking great wealth.

Psalm 119:58—(NASV)
"I sought Your favor with all my heart; Be gracious to me according to Your word."
*God's favor is something we should seek with all our hearts.

Seeking His favor on our own strength would be to miss the mark. But if we understand that favor in these verses ultimately refer to seeking His face and His presence FIRST, with all our hearts, then we can understand why God's favor is better than even gold and silver. We need to seek HIM first, to seek His face and His presence above all else, and to follow Him in love and faithfulness. Our seeking Him above all else brings His heart pleasure and His heart's response is to pour out His favor, goodness and blessings upon us.

When His favor is poured out upon us, He uses us to bring light into the darkness and to touch others with His love, His goodness and His presence. I'd like to share the following excerpt from one of my favorite authors and speakers, Graham Cooke. On his website, he posted the following article in the January Newsletter 2012: (www.grahamcooke.com)

Transformation & Favor

Affection takes a disciplined mind toward our relationship with the Holy Spirit. We have to focus our attention on Him. As Paul wrote in Colossians 3:2—"Set your mind on the things above, not on the things that are on earth." To love God, we must let our mind dwell on His nature. That makes meditation a key to intimacy. We need to think long and hard about who God is, maintaining an unbroken fellowship with Him.

"In everything give thanks; for this is God's will for you in Christ Jesus," Paul wrote in 1 Thessalonians 5:18. Intimacy has a voice—thankfulness. We need to be extremely vocal in our gratitude, practicing our thanksgiving. Real intimacy cannot be hidden because it is a transforming force. When you learn how to stay in the presence of God—to "keep yourselves in the love of God," as Jude 24 puts it—you come into favor and into the future of fulfilled prophetic words. <u>Favor rises out of the heart of God for us, and He puts us in a place of continuous blessing.</u>

God wants to transform us to look like Him. The goodness He is developing in each of us can overcome the evil that permeates throughout the world. Intimacy with God produces goodness in each of us, and that goodness can touch an entire community. What if the favor over your life is actually an umbrella that can cover an entire neighborhood, church, or even city? What if the favor on your church corporately is so large that it can cover and bless thousands of people in your town? When we, as believers, do not live in the favor of God, we allow evil to flourish around us.

Imagine a community protected and enhanced by God's favor! It all starts with Christians falling in love with Jesus and releasing His goodness to the people around them. What if God decreed that you will be so full of His presence that no one around you will be safe from a blessing? What if your role in life is to go and bless as many people as you can? What if God has marked out a specific territory for you to cover with His blessings and kindness? It is important that we explore the current level of our favor. We need to take our favor out for a spin. Just as Jesus grew in favor with both God and men, so we have to discover both of those veins of favor. God wants us to press our favor with those around us, taking as much territory for His Kingdom as possible.

May we seek His face and grow in deeper intimacy with our God. And as we do, wow! His favor will be released in greater measure over our lives and the Lord will use it to impact our families, our churches, our communities and cities. May we grow in favor with God and with all people.

Kingdom Perspective: His Pleasure

I remember listening to a teaching DVD by Lisa Bevere (when she spoke at a women's conference at IHOP in Kansas City). In this DVD, she shared about her 4 sons. She explained how she loved them all equally—but that there was 1 son in particular who had captivated her heart. Every morning, this son would wake up and the first thing he'd do was to find Lisa, no matter where she was in the house, to hug and kiss her, and to tell her "Good morning mom". He was the son who would come the first time she called. And he was the son who had a heart of loving obedience. Simply said, this particular son had won the favor of his mother's heart. Later, at a Hillsong Conference in Sydney, I had the chance to listen to John Bevere, Lisa's husband, also share about their sons. And John Bevere shared how he and Lisa would always tell their sons the following phrase: "We will always love you, no matter what. But it's up to you how much pleasure you want to bring your parents."

Anybody relate to this story? Having 3 kids, I can. That one son brought tremendous pleasure to his mother's heart. And you can imagine the favor this son had in his mother's eyes. My 3 own children are wonderful and very unique from each other. They also have the power to make their own choices. Some days, they choose to be faithful, loving and obedient. Other days, they choose to harden their hearts and become stubborn, and obstinate. I love them all equally. But when one of them chooses to listen and obey me with love, my mother's heart experiences pleasure and my heart response is to extend favor towards that child. I usually give them a big bear hug and tell them what a blessing they are to me. And as I look down into their eyes as we embrace, I see their faces and hearts smiling with joy.

When my heart experiences pleasure towards one of my children, my natural response is to have my heart so softened towards them that I extend to them my favor. I do believe we're created in the image of our loving Father and that what I experience as a mother, is a taste of the Father's heart towards his children. In Psalm 101:6, it says, *"I will look with favor on the faithful in the land, that they may dwell with me; he who walks in the way that is blameless shall minister to me."* Our Father in heaven looks with favor upon those that are faithful in the land and His desire is for these faithful ones to dwell with Him. He even says that these blameless one shall minister to Him. Wow! Lord, help us to be faithful.

As seen in Psalm 101:6, favor is given, usually as a result of our heart response to Him. Jesus loves each of us unconditionally and equally. True love is unconditional, and is explained in detail in 1 Corinthians 13. (Love is patient, kind, understanding, etc.) We are each his child, saved by grace because of the power of the cross. But it is by our choices, by our heart responses, of how much pleasure we bring to our heavenly Father and Jesus' heart. He wants to bestow favor on all of us, but what determines if His favor is released is really a result of our choices and perspectives about Him. If we truly believe that God is who He says He is and we take Him at His word of what He thinks of us (His beloved children saved by grace)and if our heart response to His love is to listen and obey His will, to be faithful, to seek wisdom and then to follow it, we will experience His favor.

If our heart response to Jesus' amazing love, grace and mercy is to not listen, not obey and not trust Him but rather to demand our own way/will and thus be disobedient, unfaithful, or even ungrateful, to not ask or seek wisdom, we will not be in the right place or position to experience God's favor and we will miss out on the honor and privilege of being a source of pleasure to His heart. We can grieve His heart or we can be a source of delight and pleasure to Him. Again, His heart's desire is to pour out His favor on ALL His children. But this is dependent on our choices and responses towards Him.

2/2/09
Journal Entry:
At 2:22 am, the following phrase hit my heart. "For your pleasure, we are created." I pondered this phrase. If our purpose was to give Him pleasure, how do we do this? And how do we show our love back to Him? As I continued to ponder this phrase, I got the following verses.

Psalm 147:11(ESV)-
"But the LORD takes pleasure in those who fear Him, in those who hope in His steadfast love."

Luke 12:32 (ESV)-
"Fear not little flock, for it is your Father's good pleasure to give you the kingdom."

Philippians 2:13 (ESV)—
"For it is God who works in you, both to will and to work for his good pleasure."

Revelations 4:11—(KJV)
"Thou art worthy, O Lord, to receive glory and honour and power; for thou has created all things, and for thy pleasure they are and were created."

In the NLT version, it says, *"You (God) created everything, and it is for your pleasure that they exist and were created."*

It's important to desire to bring the Father heart of God pleasure as His child because it is part of the purpose of why we were created by God. The word "pleasure" in this verse comes from the greek word "thelema" (thel'-ay-mah), which can be defined as "will, choice, inclination, desire, pleasure." So it was for His will, His desire and His pleasure that we were created. Ultimately, it's because He is worthy to receive all glory, honor and power from all of His creation. This includes you and me.

As I end my personal study on favor and pleasure, perhaps this concept can best be understood through Mary, the mother of Jesus.

Luke 1: 26-33 (ESV)
"In the sixth month the angel Gabriel was sent from God to a city of Galilee named Nazareth, to a virgin betrothed to a man whose name was Joseph, of the house of David. And the virgin's name was Mary. And he came to her and said, "Greetings, O favored one, the Lord is with you!" But she was greatly troubled at the saying, and tried to discern what sort of greeting this might be. And the angel said to her, "Do not be afraid, Mary, for you have found favor with God. And behold, you will conceive in your womb and bear a son, and you shall call his name Jesus. He will be great and will be called the Son of the Most High. And the Lord God will give

to him the throne of his father David, and he will reign over the house of Jacob forever, and of his kingdom there will be no end."

Mary is called "O favored one" by the angel Gabriel. Wow! She gets to be the mother of Jesus. That blows my mind! And she gets to spend all eternity honored by God and by all the saints as the mother of Jesus! What favor!

But let's think about her life on Earth. Once pregnant, she risked getting stoned by a people that didn't believe she was carrying the son of God in her womb and believed she had a child out of wedlock. Her betrothed bridegroom at first also didn't believe she was carrying the Son of God in her womb. So God had to get his attention through dreams. Then Mary had to ride a donkey during her final trimester of her first pregnancy through difficult terrain, and then had to give birth in a cave, filled with animals (which means there was manure and very earthy smells and noises while she gave birth for the first time). On top of that, she was just a teen, newly married. After her son was born, she and her husband had to move to a foreign country because her young child's life was in danger. Eventually, she and her husband had many children together after Jesus but then her husband died and she was left to raise all of them on her own. Then, she had to watch her oldest son Jesus get mocked by the crowds, captured and tortured by Roman soldiers and killed horrifically on a cross.

The favor of God doesn't equate to an Americanized view of a life of riches, power, fame and a life of ease—free from suffering. The favor of God means His face and His presence will be upon you, as you walk through life, through the good times as well as those times of deep sorrow and even suffering.

Chapter 11
Keys of the Kingdom of Heaven

Have you ever thought about keys? You know . . . that piece of metal we use to open our house door to enter our homes, to get into our cars, or even to unlock a vault to get the treasure inside. Keys are something we often take for granted. Sometimes, we even treat them as a nuisance to carry. "It's too heavy!" "It stabs my legs when I carry them in my pocket!" "It's so hard to find in my purse!" We even complain when it's hard to put a key into a keyhole and turn that lock. But if we were to lock our keys in the car, forget our house keys to get into our homes, or misplace our car keys so we can't start our cars, our entire perspective on keys instantly shifts and keys are now very vital! We would instantly see the importance of having keys in our possession so that we can use them to open the locked doors and have access to the things we need.

In the kingdom of God, there are also keys.

Matthew 16:19 (NIV) says, "I will give you the keys of the kingdom of heaven; whatever you bind on earth will be bound in Heaven, and whatever you loose on earth will be loosed in Heaven."

I don't know why He created keys of the kingdom of heaven. But I do know they exist. In my times of being still and listening to Jesus, I have been shown some things about keys to His kingdom. This may be simply for me personally. But out of obedience to Him, I am sharing these things with you. Ultimately, I pray He would breathe His Breath of Life (in Hawaiian we call it His Ha) on the things He desires to reveal to you and that His will would be accomplished.

7/29/06
Journal Entry:

Tonight I had a wonderful time of just being in Your presence, waiting silently before You with Dwight. Dwight was sitting on the edge of the bed and I was on my knees. We waited on You, praying and waiting in silence. Later Dwight went outside to pray more in the living room. I stayed on my knees in the bedroom to wait more. As I was waiting, I saw bright lights coming down from the ceiling. I was then told to open my hands and asked to look at them. I strained my eyes and I thought I saw a little bit of red in the center. I asked God for help to see more clearly. I put my hands close and looked. I could see an outline of a key, white in color in my hands. It was light in the shape of a key. I gasped as my eyes wide open saw this key in my hands. I quickly closed my hands and said, "Thanks! I receive it!" But then I stopped and asked the LORD, "What is this key for? Immediately I got 2 verses: Isaiah 22:22 (NIV), *"I will place on his shoulder the key to the house of David; what he opens no one can shut, and what he shuts no one can open."* And Revelations 3:8 (ESV), *"I know your works. Behold, I have set before you an open door, which no one is able to shut. I know that you have but little power, and yet you have kept my word and have not denied my name."*

3/16/08-
Journal Entry:

Keys are used to unlock doors and to help us enter through doors into new environments.

3/28/08
Journal Entry:

It's 3 a.m.

This morning, I was spending time in Your presence. I felt You impress upon my heart to hold out my hands. So I did. With my eyes closed, I saw a whole bunch of keys placed into my hands. For some reason, the keys on my left hand felt heavier than the keys on my right hand. I prayed to Jesus for help with using these keys. All of a sudden I saw little red hearts floating down from heaven upon these keys. I knew instantly that You were giving me love to use these keys with. Thank you Jesus.

Keys intrigue me Lord. Holy Spirit, please help and reveal to me what they are and what/how/when etc. to use these keys. Thank You Jesus!

Kingdom Perspective:
The Key of Communion-

3/21/08
Journal Entry:

Tonight as a dear friend and I were praying and waiting in silence before the Lord, I began to be filled with gratitude and thanksgiving as I thought about Jesus and the cross. Immediately the verse, "We shall enter His gates with thanksgiving in our hearts, we shall enter His courts with praise" (Psalm 100:4), popped into my mind. The Holy Spirit then prompted me to move to my favorite spot in the old Elevate church building. As I knelt on the floor, instantly I could see in my mind, someone walking down a flight of stairs with a HUGE key in his hands. I was told by Jesus to hold out my hands. As the key was placed into my hands, I could immediately feel that the key was heavy. Then I felt prompted by His Spirit to bring the key to my heart. I tried to physically move my hands up but I couldn't lift it any higher. I giggled as I tried harder to lift the key. I was amazed that I couldn't do it. Jesus then told me to ask my friend to help me. She had left the main room so I waited. As soon as I saw she was within ear range, I asked, "Hey, can you help me?" She saw me on the floor with my hands opened. As she knelt beside me and reached out her hands next to mine to help me lift, she immediately exclaimed, "Wow! What is this? It's heavy!" We both laughed. I told her, "It's a huge key and I need your help to lift it to my heart." So the 2 of us struggled to lift it together to my heart. When we finally got the key up and into my heart, the weight immediately was gone from my hands. The Lord then showed me what the key was. Written in huge letters on this enormous key was the word "COMMUNION." And as I asked the Lord about it, this is the revelation He gave me.

When you take communion (the bread and the wine), you do this in remembrance of Me. As you remember Me, just as you did tonight, your heart is then filled with thankfulness for the cross and for the grace that saved you from your sins. Psalm 100:4 states that a thankful heart helps you enter into the gates of My spiritual Kingdom. As you continue in worship and praise of Me, this helps you enter into My courts. This is the heart behind why I ask you to take communion, so that we can commune together and so that you can be in My presence.

Kingdom Perspective:
The Key of Resurrection Power
And the Key of Hebrews 11:1 (The Key of Faith)

2/21/09-
Journal Entry:

Another friend and I had the most amazing time, waiting on the Lord together. We both got the same directions from Jesus as we waited in silence. "Go to the front of the building." As we got to the front threshold, we dropped to our knees. Both of us sensed the Lord had a key for us and was teaching us about faith tonight.

We didn't know how to get it. So we waited in silence. I felt prompted by the Spirit to speak out the following. So I did. I opened my mouth and said, "Believing this is you Jesus, I command the ground to uncover the key." My friend saw the key first. As I looked, I could see it too. I was instructed to pick it up. And as I did, my hands SHOOK!! She then saw it grow in size. I sensed it was a very powerful. I asked the Lord to show me what it was for. And then I saw the words "RESURRECTION POWER" written on it.

As we held the large key in our hands, we both fell over. The key contained that much power! He then led us to another area in our church building. Once there, my friend saw a door in the spirit. She sensed that we needed to use the key to open this door. As I took the large key, my hands again shook really hard. And by faith, I put the key into the door and it opened. The Lord led us through the doorway and into a passageway. We were led on quite a journey, but as we pressed on to the end of it, we both felt a surge of power and elation. I felt like jumping up and down in victory. So I did. Then I felt the LORD wanted me to yell something 3 times. So I obeyed. "VICTORY IS THE LORD'S!" I yelled from the depths of my being. At that point, my friend fell over as she was hit by the power of God. I then began to declare prophetic declarations as I heard them directly from Him. The first one had to do with horses. She could hear their hoof prints. The 2nd one I can't remember. Then the 3rd one was about the watchmen to arise in the high places.

Many more things happened that I was not permitted to share but at the end, Jesus told me to get a scroll. I asked my friend if she saw a scroll. It was a confirmation as she described what she saw, exactly the same scroll that I could see in my hands. He told me to open it. As I looked at the scroll with greater scrutiny, I noticed some very small writing that I had not noticed before. As I looked, I saw a thin (dotted?) line written across the scroll. And across that line was the word "FAITH" with Hebrews 11:1 written underneath the line.

Hebrews 11:1 (NASB)
"Now faith is the assurance of things hoped for and the conviction of things not seen."

Romans 10:17 (NASB) also came to mind.
"So faith comes from hearing, and hearing by the word of Christ."

Then this was revelatory. As I sat there pondering why this was on the scroll, I got the following.

"Faith comes from hearing, but not necessarily from the logos word of God, but rather the rhema (living word) of God. The word of God becomes rhema when it is filled with the power and anointing of the Holy Spirit. Faith ultimately comes from hearing Jesus."

04/01/09
Journal Entry:

As I sat in my bed after waking up, I looked up and said, "Good Morning Jesus." Immediately Jesus spoke. You need to write today Liza. Get that key. In my spirit I knew immediately the key He was referring to—the key of Faith. I watched as I saw this key immediately grow in size in my hands. Then I needed 2 hands to hold it. It grew really big, over 2 feet long in my hands. And the words FAITH were written on it.

As I held the key in my hands, it became a bridge. And I saw others with keys in their hands. Some keys were really big—and as one young man held out his key, it became a bridge as big as the San Francisco Golden Gate Bridge. Jesus explained. "Liza, as you use your faith, your key of faith will grow into a bridge." As I looked at my bridge, it was so small compared to the one that particular young man had. And I felt a bit intimidated and sheepish. "Liza, I give to each child of mine, a key of faith. Every child has one—but to each is allotted a particular size. Do not compare your faith to others. But you are responsible for what you have been given. Activate your faith. Remember Hebrews 11:1. As you step out in obedience and faithfulness to the things I tell you and ask, your key of faith will grow. The reason faith grows into a bridge is because of its purpose. Part of the purpose of this bridge is ultimately to bring the lost to Me."

I felt relieved that I needed to just focus on Jesus and be faithful with what He had given me and that He didn't expect me to be like anyone else.

10/07/09
Journal Entry:
Waiting on the Lord in silence. You knew that I had been struggling with doubt . . . again. Then You reminded me of "Faith" and of what You had recently shown me in a vision. In it, I saw You write on the palms of my hands. On my left palm was inscribed the words, "You are Mine" and on the right, "Believe."

Then the Lord told me to hold out my hands. I could see other hands there as well. Each of us had been given different portions of faith. Then He spoke. "Do not compare yourself to others. Be faithful with what you've been given. Learn and be encouraged by the faith of others, and in doing so, your faith will grow. Faith comes from hearing, and hearing from the Word of God. I am the Word. I AM Jesus."

*Kingdom Perspective:
The key of a Pure Heart

Psalm 24:3-6 (ESV)
"Who shall ascend the hill of the LORD? And who shall stand in His holy place? He who has clean hands and a pure heart, who does not lift up his soul to what is false and does not swear deceitfully. He will receive blessing from the LORD & righteousness from the God of His salvation. Such is the generation of those who seek Him, who seek the face of Jacob."

11/27/09
Journal Entry:

Tonight, as my friend and I were soaking and waiting on the Lord while we lay on the stage floor, she was told to sit up and turn around. I was told to remain on my back with my eyes closed. Then we both saw doors. We compared what revelation we received from the Lord and interestingly, we realized it was a door to the North and a door to the South.

The door I saw divided into 2 parts. So if you opened the door, it would open up in the middle with the 2 halves opening up to each side. The door was white and very elegant looking. My friend saw her door white as well. As I looked at the door, I heard the Lord say "You need to open the door." As I looked at it, I had no clue how to open it. "Use one of the keys I already gave you", He replied. Suddenly, I saw a most beautiful white elegant key. It looked like it was made out of white porcelain. As I looked closer at the key, I saw the words "Pure Heart" engraved on it. The Lord then reminded me that it was only because of His blood that made my heart pure. Then the Lord told me to ask my friend what she saw. She started to describe the key to me as being red in color and with a tiny white heart attached to it. I then shared with her what I saw and about the power of His blood that made our hearts pure. We were amazed at how creative Jesus was.

He then told me to pick it up. So I did. The key was heavy and as I grabbed it, it grew in size in my hands. Now it was about 8 inches long. "Now what Lord?" I asked. "There's only 1 key, but there's 2 of us. In my heart, I thought if I gave my friend the key, what would happen if I wouldn't have a key to open my door. "Lord, what am I supposed to do? Please give me wisdom." Again, I stared back at the key that I was holding in my right hand. "Lord do you want me to give it to her?" As I looked at His face, He didn't say "yes" or "no". He simply looked back at me. "Lord, do you want me to pray to make a copy of the key?" In my heart, I thought that was a pretty creative idea but as I looked at His face, I could see Him looking intently at me as if He was studying my heart and motives. And He still didn't reply. "Lord, what do you want me to do?" Then He spoke. "Give her the key." All of a sudden, I realized how small my view of His nature was. How could I have doubted His goodness? I gave my friend the key, and immediately after I did, I found another identical white key in my right hand. Jesus then spoke to me with a smile. "As a leader, you will be tempted to hold on to the very treasures that I have given to you. But you need to freely give what has been given to you (to those that I tell you to invest in). As you do, you will never lose these treasures. Your ceiling is their floor." Immediately I was relieved because I sensed I had just passed another test.

The Lord then directed both of us to stand up and go to each door. My friend headed to the back of the building. I headed to the front.

As I stood before the white door that I could now see in the North facing wall, I was reminded of the importance of having child-like faith. "Help me to be like a child Jesus", I prayed. As I scanned the door, I looked at the top of the door for any labels. Immediately the Lord told me that I wouldn't find any written words at the top. All of sudden, as I looked at the middle of the door, I saw the word "ENTER" appear in big capital letters across the middle.

I put my 2 hands to the key, put it in the keyhole and turned it. Then I felt the key unlock the door. Suddenly the door started to open. It was interesting to watch because it looked like parts of the door were opening up in a beautiful pattern.

As I saw the scenery behind the door unveil before me, I simply gasped. It was so beautiful. I saw waterfalls, beautiful green meadows and flowing streams. Tranquil, breath taking, and peaceful, I wanted so badly to bolt through that door and enter this delightful place. Then the Lord said to look down. As I looked down, I realized there was a doormat on the floor right before the door. And written in big black letters across it were the words "MY REST." "Ooooohhhhhhh. Enter My Rest! I get it Lord!!" I got so excited by this revelation. A pure heart before the Lord is a key to entering the Lord's Rest. When we come to Him in true repentance, His blood totally cleans our hearts and they are now pure before Him. As we rest in our identity of who we are, sealed by His blood because Christ is in us because of the cross, we confidently can approach His throne of grace and enter His rest. No striving in our flesh—simply resting in Him, confident of our place before Him because we believe that He is who He says He is and we are who He says we are—His beloved child.

Then Jesus spoke. "Liza, this is My place of Rest. This is what you see before your eyes." As I stood there, I suddenly felt like I was being covered with a heavy warm blanket of peace. I felt so peaceful and restful. And I didn't want to move. "Jesus, please give me a pure heart. I want to enter Your Rest and be in this place all the time." And in my heart, I now knew that I could enter this place any time, as long as I had a pure heart before Him.

Matthew 5:8 (ESV)—*"Blessed are the **pure in heart**, for they shall see God."*

1 Timothy 1:5 (ESV)—*"But the goal of our **in**struction is love from a **pure heart** and a good conscience and a sincere faith."*

More Kingdom Keys:

Over a period of about 3 months, the Lord began to show me 12 keys that were all attached to a bracelet. I don't understand why He chose to use this analogy with me. But as I prayed about this manuscript, I felt I was supposed to include this in the book. I pray that whatever the Lord desires to reveal, confirm, encourage or impart to you would be accomplished. May His will be done.

Key of Persistent Prayer

10/15/09
Journal Entry:
I could see in the spirit, a bracelet Jesus had given to me at one of our soaking nights at church. Another dear young man who was part of our church family saw in the spirit the bracelet on my wrist right after Jesus had given it to me. He described what he saw to me and I smiled as it was a total confirmation to what I saw.

The bracelet was transparent and made out of diamonds. There were links in the bracelet. I was told that each one represented links that would be included in this book. I also

115

saw keys on it. The keys were really small, like the size of charms on a regular bracelet. I was told to count the keys on the bracelet. I counted 12, including the 1 key that was part of the clasp, holding the entire bracelet together.

Jesus told me that when people would read and examine these keys, they would be healed.

As I looked at the bracelet, I examined the first key I saw. I saw "per" written in flames. The letters were gold colored on the key. I looked closer. The word was "persistent". As I asked the Lord about it, I was impressed with the following:

Persistent prayer
Persistent peace
Persistent perseverance

Later, I was reading the bible & Romans 12:12 really caught my heart. *"Rejoice in hope; be patient in affliction; be persistent in prayer. "(Holman Christian Standard Bible)*

Key of Humility and the key of Honor

10/23/09
Journal Entry:

This morning, my left hand began to shake again. I knew it had to do with the bracelet. As I looked at the bracelet, this time I couldn't see as clearly. I don't know why. Then I saw a key that looked ancient and aged. I then saw Jesus raise his hand and lift 2 fingers up. "Two?" I responded. I looked more closely. There was another key connected to the ancient one. But this key was transparent and clear. I asked the Lord if I could take it off the bracelet and put it in the palm of my left hand. He nodded "yes" so I did. Suddenly Dwight, who was lying in bed next to me still half asleep, felt my left hand brush against his and he then held my left hand. "Oh oh!" I thought, "the keys!" Suddenly in the spirit, I could see keyholes forming in my open left palm and in Dwight's right open palm. I looked closer. Then I watched as the antique key went to the lock in Dwight's palm and the clear key went into mine. The keys turned and opened the locks. It was a perfect fit!!

Then I was given the names for these keys. The ancient antique looking key that fit into the keyhole on Dwight's palm was "Humility." The clear key that fit into mine was "Honor." Then I was given the revelation that these 2 keys opened the doors to deeper intimacy in marriage relationships.

Key of Relentless Obedience-

10/27/09
Journal Entry:

My left hand started shaking. Then I was instructed to look at the bracelet again.

At first, I couldn't see any key in this particular section. Then I spotted something really small. As I looked closely, I found a very tiny pink key. I asked the Lord why it was so small. I got the word "breathe". "What? Breath on it?" I replied. At first I thought I was suppose to breathe on the key but when I checked with wisdom, the answer was "no". Then I saw Jesus extend His hand to me. "Give the key to me". So I did. I watched as He breathed on it and right before my eyes, it supernaturally grew huge! Then He gave this big pink key back to me.

I realized now that this key was in the shape of the cross. I was instructed to look at it closely. As I did, I looked for a name/ word on it. At first, all I could see was the letter "R". Then I saw "Re", then "Rel". I had to keep looking and looking until I finally got the 1st word—"Relentless". It was written in gold and had diamonds embedded in it. I continued to look with the lens. Then I saw the 2nd word—"Obedience". It was also written in gold with diamonds embedded in it. As I pondered what this meant, I was got the phrase "PURE HEART." Then I heard the following. "It takes a pure heart to see and find this one key. Many miss it because it's so small. To be relentless in obedience is impossible apart from Jesus. The only way to do this is for Him to literally breath His life and Spirit upon you."

Key of being a Child of God

12/08/09
Continuation of journal entry:

Later on, as I continued to soak, the Lord brought my attention back to my bracelet as my left hand shook and shook. I could see a purple key that was the main latch holding the bracelet together as the bracelet shook. And Jesus had a huge smile on his face. He really liked this key. As I looked at it, I could see the phrase "Child of God" written on it. No wonder it was the main key holding this bracelet together.

Keys of Peace and Zoe

12/12/09
Journal Entry:

My left hand started shaking again. I knew immediately He wanted to reveal more things to me about the bracelet. I got the word "Innocence" so I asked the Lord what this meant. I was instructed to look again. Over this word written very small was the verse Colossians 3:11.

Col 3:11—(NASB)
"a renewal in which there is no distinction between Greek and Jew, circumcised and uncircumcised, barbarian, Scythian, slave and freeman, but Christ is all, and in all."

Later, I looked up the word innocence on my laptop. And in an online dictionary, the definition of innocence included: 1) the state of not being guilty of a crime or offense and 2) freedom from sin or evil.

Then I got the word "PURENESS" and there was a verse from Isaiah written on it. But for some reason, I was not clear on what the exact chapter and verse were.

In the Merriam Webster dictionary, pureness was defined as: 1) unmixed with any other matter (pure gold); free from dust, dirt, or taint (pure springwater); spotless, stainless; free from harshness or roughness and being in tune 2) free from what violates, weakens, or pollutes; containing nothing that does not properly belong; free from moral fault or guilt; marked by chastity.

I asked Him why He gave me these 2 words. He then explained that when I had a heart of innocence and pureness (all done through the cleansing power of the powerful blood of Jesus), my heart would then reflect His heart—one of total pureness and innocence. When I had a heart like His, I would be able to see people and situations the way that He saw them. In other words, I would have His heart perspective.

As I waited with my physical eyes closed, I suddenly could feel the gentle breeze of the Holy Spirit against my face. It was so sweet feeling His presence.

Then He instructed me to look at the bracelet again. As I looked, I could see the bracelet looking brighter and clearer to me. I could also see the transparent links and the purple key that was the main clasp that held the bracelet together labeled "Child of God." As I shook my hand, the bracelet shook and the little keys on it shook as well. I could see the pink one. As I turned my wrist again, I then saw an orange and a green key.

I was instructed to look at the orange key first. On it was written the word "peace." Right after I got that word, immediately I felt His peace like a warm blanket cover me. It felt warm and peaceful.

Jesus then told me peace comes when we surrender. He showed me what that hospital room looked like, the night before my firstborn son Koby was born. I could see myself sitting up in my hospital bed with my arms stretched out in worship. And I saw the Father on the throne looking down and Jesus standing before me. And as I saw myself with tears streaming down my cheeks singing in worship to Jesus and surrendering my son's life to Him, I watched as the room filled with an orange glow and His spirit of peace covered me. And I was so grateful.

Then He instructed me to look at the green key. It looked emerald green in color & marble in texture. I asked the Lord what was written on it. He told me "It starts with a Z." "Z?" I was intrigued. Then I saw it. "ZOE." Immediately, I felt the intense power of the Holy Spirit and knew this key was very powerful. Then He told me that many don't have this key yet but in His last day's army, every soldier would possess one of these zoe keys.

I asked Jesus who had this key before. And He replied "Enoch".

Way off in the distance to my left, I saw a man waving to me. He had a green key in his hand and immediately I knew it was Enoch. Then I heard, "This green key is released to those who walk in deep intimacy with Me."

Keys of Confession, Promises, Daddy's kid/Father's love

My left hand started to shake once more. I knew it was time to look for another key. Jesus gave me a "thumbs up." So I brought the bracelet up to my eyes to look. I saw 3 more keys. The first one was aquamarine. The body of the key was clear blue. It was so pretty. The next key was clear yellow. The last key was really interesting. It was purple and white.

He told me to look at the aquamarine key. I then took it off the bracelet and put it on my hand. That's when I realized I forgot to check with Jesus and ask Him if this was what He wanted me to do. I immediately told Jesus I was sorry for not waiting and inquiring of Him first before placing the key into my palm. All of a sudden, the blue key in my hand released what looked like light blue illuminated liquid. I immediately felt so clean and good inside. Then I looked at the key closely. I asked the Lord what type of key it was. He told me it began with the letter "c". All of a sudden, I saw the word "confession" on it. And then I understood what just happened. When I had repented and confessed my sin of being presumptuous and not inquiring of Him first, my heartfelt confession to Jesus allowed me to receive His cleaning power.

Thank you Jesus for the gift of confession!

Then it was time to look at the yellow key. Right at this point, Kailee, my youngest daughter jumped into bed next to me as I was waiting on the Lord. I told her I needed to spend time with Jesus. At that point, I looked to the Lord and He said to stop and love on her. So I did. Then as I continued to wait, He instructed me to take off the yellow key, put into my hand and ask Kailee what she saw. So I did. Kailee looked at my hand and then said "I see a heart—a big heart!" "What color is it?" I asked. She responded, "It's rainbow colored. It has a happy face on it and a heart face. I see pictures on it. I see lots of happy faces—people's faces, a dog face, a family's faces, a cat face." I was intrigued. Then she ran off to the next room. I then asked Jesus "Why did Kailee see a rainbow heart instead of a yellow key?"

Jesus replied. "The color yellow represents the sun. All light on Earth comes from the sun. But light as you see it is actually made up of multi colors, thus the rainbow colored heart that your daughter saw." I looked at the yellow key again. This time I saw the word "Promises" engraved in gold letters upon the yellow key. Jesus responded. "This yellow color represents me—the SON. I am also the Word of Truth. I have spoken and declared many promises in My written word. My promises are like steel beams in a structure. They are meant to provide support. And when the storms come, My promises, just like steel beams and steel hinges (like steel hurricane protection stuff), will help support you and strengthen you through it. So stand on My promises!"

"Why did Kailee see a heart?" I asked. "Because My promises have been given to you out of My heart of love. The truth is I love you and I've promised I will be with you, even until the end of the age. Love will never fail because I AM love. And I will never fail."

"Jesus, why did Kailee see so many happy faces, including a dog and a cat?" He quickly answered with a smile. "Kailee's concept of a family includes pets. You have a rabbit and 2 dogs. Many of her friends have cats as pets. I love families. I, along with My Father, desired to have a family. That's why I died on the cross. For the joy set before Me. Part of My joy came because I knew my sacrifice would allow us to have a family forever with you and with all those that have called and will call upon My name to be saved."

I thought immediately of the color yellow and how joy many times is associated with that color. Jesus knew my thoughts. He responded, "Yes, yellow many times represents joy. You see, the joy that was set before Me as I went to the cross was you, and all those that are Mine." I was so deeply touched that we were that valued and loved by Jesus. What amazing love!

I was ready to move on to the next key but then I saw Jesus put up 1 finger. "One more thing" he said. I stopped and listened. I have thousands of promises in My written word. Yet many of my children do not stand on them. Tell them to "STAND on my promises. The clock is ticking. There isn't much time left before I return."

At that point, I got the following picture. I saw soldiers in God's army taking out their swords and plunging them into solid ground. Then they attached themselves to their swords to help them stand.

Then I saw one soldier close up. He was being attacked by the enemy and his forces. I saw the words "fear", "lust" and "perversion" identifying what was attacking him. As the enemy tried to strike, he held up His shield of faith. Interestingly, I also saw bright yellow light come from the solid ground, pass through the sword, through his body and then illuminate the shield. And he was able to stand firm and also remained untouched and unharmed by the enemy's strike against him.

Jesus replied, "Liza, I AM the Rock. Do you see now what happens when you stand on My promises in My written word with faith? So STAND!" I felt such intense power when He spoke this. "Jesus, help me to stand with faith in You!"

Then it was time to look at the next key. This one was interesting to look at. It was solid in color, not transparent like the other 2 keys. It kept changing from a purple background covered with white dots to a white background with purple spots. I was curious. Why was it changing backgrounds? Why were there dots? And why was it colored purple and white?

He replied, "It's changing because it really is 2 keys in 1." "Cool!" I thought. But then I realized I had no clue what He meant by this. I looked at the key in my hand. Right now, it had a purple background with white dots. "What is this key Jesus?" "It begins with a 'D'." I still had no clue what this word was. I looked at the key again. Then I saw 2 letters. "DA." I still was clueless. Then I saw the phrase "Daddy's girl/boy." He continued.

"The purple background represents "royalty." That's who you are because you are the Father's child. All those that truly know Me are sons and daughters of the Most High God. That makes you of royal lineage. Dots are circular in shape. There's no end or beginning point in a circular band like a simple gold ring. It's continuous and never ending. This represents My love for you—continuous and never ending."

Then I saw the key change into the one with a white background with purple dots. On the key was written "The Father's Love." He explained. "It is colored white because I AM. I AM pure, holy and just. And My love for you is pure, holy, and just. I AM the King of Kings. Therefore all glory belongs to Me. I AM royalty. This is represented by the purple dots."

I thought about this and replied, "I still don't get the dots Lord. I get the purple color but not the dots." Jesus told me to take a closer look at the dots. So I did. As I looked, I saw moving pictures in these purple dots. In one of them, Jesus was healing somebody. In another, Jesus was on the cross. In another He was on His white horse as the Lord of Hosts. "These dots are simply glimpses of who I AM. You will not see Me in all My fullness until you see Me face to face as I am on My judgment seat."

When I heard "judgment seat" my mouth said "Whoa!" Then He smiled. "Liza, don't forget My judgment seat is the same as My mercy seat. I judge because I love. And I am merciful, righteous and just."

"Why did You say this is really 2 keys in 1?" I asked. "Because child, you cannot have one without the other. They work together as 1 powerful key. The Father loves you, because you belong to Him. You are His child. But if you don't receive the Father's love, you will not believe in your heart that you are truly Daddy's girl or boy—basically His beloved child. When you hear Daddy's girl or Daddy's boy, it is a human term of endearment. Beloved, you are dear to your Father in heaven. All of His children need to know their identity in Christ. He loves you. This is related to that purple key I showed you earlier that was the clasp of this bracelet—'A child of God'."

I was then instructed to pick up this 2 in 1 key. I then saw a door in front of me. On the door was the label "Promises." He instructed me to put the key in the lock. So I did. As I turned it, the door opened and bright yellow light illuminated out. And as I sat and pondered these things, I realized how many of these keys were interrelated.

Jesus, thank you for this time. I pray for an increase of Your spirit of revelation and wisdom and that You would give me illumination and understanding of the things You've shown me tonight. I love you Jesus!

The Destiny Image Key and the Oil Key

12/18/09
Journal Entry:

This morning, the Lord showed me the last 2 keys on the bracelet. My left hand started to shake. As I looked at the bracelet, I could see a small white key. As I looked closer, I saw that it had a mirror as part of the key. On the key was written the phrase "Destiny Image" in white letters. Even though the key was already white, I still could see the white letters engraved upon it. As I brought the key closer, I noticed blood flowing down from the key. Immediately I knew that this represented the blood of Jesus. As I gazed into the mirror on the key, I was expecting to see myself. I was surprised that as I looked into this special mirror, I saw Jesus hanging on the cross. I asked the Lord why I saw this. He told me it was my destiny to look and be like Jesus in this world. That meant I needed to learn to die to myself. He told me to look more closely at the key. As I did, I saw Galatians 2:20 written on the bottom of the mirror on the key. "I have been crucified with Christ . . ."

Now I knew why I had seen blood flowing from this key. It was only by His blood that this could supernaturally happen.

The second and final key He wanted to show me was a small gold key. As I looked at it, I asked the Lord what it was. He gave me the letter "O". I looked at the key. This time I could see the letters "O" and "K". "OK? Is that it?" I was wondering what that meant. Then I was told to look again. As I did, I saw the following. Next to the letter "O" in smaller letters were written "il" and next to the "K" were written "EY." "Oil Key?" I said out loud, wondering what He meant by that. As I prayed, I got the phrase "Oil of Gladness." Immediately I thought of Isaiah 61.

Isaiah 61:3
"and provide for those who grieve in Zion— to bestow on them a crown of beauty instead of ashes, the oil of gladness instead of mourning, and a garment of praise instead of a spirit of despair. They will be called oaks of righteousness, a planting of the LORD for the display of his splendor."

As I looked at the gold key, I noticed oil dripping from it. I asked the Lord what this key was for. I was shown a beautiful ornate bottle filled with oil. This key was then taken to this bottle and there was a lock on it. I didn't know why. Then I was told to put the key into the lock. So I did. And as I did, oil began to flow from this bottle.

Later, He poured some of the oil from this vial over me. Wow, I felt happy and glad inside. This oil of gladness was powerful and lifted my spirit. It was nice!

All of a sudden, I could see the cloud of witnesses. They started to gather around in a circle. I was part of the circle. Then Jesus came and asked me for the bracelet with the 12 keys on it. I quickly stuck my left arm out. He smiled. As He took off the bracelet from my arm and held it in His hand, He was smiling. As I took my left hand back, I was happily surprised to find an exact bracelet on my left hand replacing the one I had just freely given to Him. He reminded me that I could never out give Him.

Then the bracelet was placed on the floor in the middle of the circle. He told me to speak the command "Multiply." I felt so unworthy but I obeyed because I knew it was only because of His blood and power that I could do any of this. As I spoke that word, I was amazed to see a huge pile of bracelets (for the women) and key rings with the same 12 keys (for the men) appear instantly before my eyes. Everyone was so excited. Then the Lord spoke and said that these keys were for every single soldier in His Last Days army.

Kingdom Perspective:
Bow and Arrows

08/12/09
Journal Entry:

I stayed up through the night—trying to wait, hear God, and press in. I read a bit from Francis Frangipane's book-This Day We Fight. And I read about the bow Francis was given.

All of a sudden I sensed an angel to the left of the bed holding a bow. But I struggled if I should receive it. (Once again, my eyes were focused on myself and not Jesus.) I felt doubt, discouragement and depression fill the room. Suddenly, I took the authority God had given me and commanded these things to leave. Immediately, the atmosphere cleared. Thank you Lord!

Then I was told to stand. I could see the line in the ground and then heard, "Choose this day whom you will serve." I stepped over the line, again. Then in the late morning, Jesus spoke.

"It's time to receive the bow Liza." I was told to hold my hands out. So I did. Then I was surprised because instead of being given a bow, I received arrows. They were so beautifully crafted. They were made of silver metal and had engravings on them that said "Arrows of Truth." Immediately, I thought to myself, "Hey, these arrows can be used against the enemy and also for those that are blinded prisoners."

Suddenly the Lord stuck His hand out right in front of my face. "Stop!" He boomed. I thought "oh oh, I'm in trouble now." Jesus intently looked at me. "Liza, these arrows are to fight the enemy. They are not to be used against My children—not in the way you are thinking." I immediately repented.

Thankfully, He continued to speak. "Your book and what you are walking through right now will help multiply arrows in the hands of your fellow warriors. There is purpose—My purpose—in why I allowed you to walk through this painful experience. It wasn't an accident." Suddenly, I saw a bigger picture and understanding of what He wanted to accomplish through my journey.

Then He instructed me to hold out my left hand and grab the case to hold the arrows in. It was beautiful and had a dark wine color. I was told to put the arrows in it and then sling it over my left arm and hang it over my left shoulder so that it would rest on my back.

Then He told me to hold out my hands again. This time He placed the bow on it. It was silver. I heard the word "titanium." The Lord said it would never break. On it was written the words "My God is faithful and true." He reminded me also of 2 Timothy 2:13 (NASB). "If we are faithless, He remains faithful, for He cannot deny Himself."

Then He told me to get an arrow. I got the phrase "Target Practice." I asked Him for help for I had no clue how to do this. "Listen to the Holy Spirit." So I grabbed an arrow and listened. "Stick out your pointer finger"(my left hand that was holding the bow upright). So I did. "Put the tip of the arrow on your pointer." So I did. "Pull back (the arrow)." So I did. "Point forward . . . higher . . . higher . . . higher . . . to the left . . . a little more . . . okay now! Let it go." As I released the arrow, I could see the target in the distance. And I saw an angel leading the arrow to the target. Jesus said, "When you listen and follow the Holy Spirit's leading, these arrows will always hit the target." Then He said, "Look at what happens when you shoot the arrows without His leading." I then saw some arrows being launched from bows without the Holy Spirit's leading. They flew in the sky. But they landed without hitting the intended target. Worse, a few hit some prisoners, and ended up wounding them even more. Then I saw the enemy's forces picking up some of the arrows that landed on the ground and then using them to stab and accuse and condemn the brethren.

*Kingdom Perspective:
The Cloak of Humility-

10/08/09
Journal Entry:

As I was waking up this morning, I put on my spiritual armor. When I was putting on the cloak of humility over the armor, I noticed 2 round pins/brooches on it. He had given these to me months before to clip the cloak on. I had simply seen them as pretty and shiny. This time however, my attention was drawn to it. I was told to look at it. So I did.

On the round pin/brooch on my left shoulder, I saw the word "Truth" written in beautiful script. It was the largest word engraved onto it and was the focal word. But there were smaller phrases/words written in different fonts on the pin/ brooch. I saw "about me", "about God", and "about others." I think there were other smaller words printed on it as well but I couldn't read them. Then I was instructed to look at the other round pin/brooch on my right shoulder. So I did. I saw an eye on it. Then I heard Him say, "My eyes see everything. It is wisdom to fear Me. The eye also represents your need to see as I do. It should always be your goal to see Me and recognize Me in others, regardless of their outward appearance." I pondered these things as I thought about how these pins/brooches were used to hold the cloak of humility over my shoulders and back.

Chapter 12
In These End Times . . .

*Kingdom Perspective:
It's Time to Ride

6/23/06
Journal Entry:

At a meeting in May, as Dwight and I were praying, I kept "hearing" in my spirit—"It's time to ride" over and over again.

7/11/06
Journal Entry:

The other night, you put Isaiah 40:3 (ESV) on my heart.

A voice cries: "In the wilderness prepare the way of the LORD; Make straight in the desert a highway for our God."

Again, you put this verse on my heart. I waited on God. Between 3 and 3:39 a.m. You spoke. And in my mind, I saw, in my left hand, a torch. In my right hand, I held a sword and I was riding a horse. My sword was still small (humble pie) but He told me that I needed to wield it and as I did, it would grow. The torch was regular in size but in time, He said it would grow and increase and increase, all for God's glory. I begged God for wisdom and humility.

7/24/06
Journal Entry:

We are in war. The battle is on. We war not against flesh and blood but against principalities, powers, rulers of the darkness of this age, spiritual hosts of wickedness in the heavenly places.

I had a radical time of being silent before the Lord and waiting in His presence. I saw bright lights descending from heaven into our bedroom. I also saw a hole in the ceiling. And through the hole I could see a dark blue night sky with stars.

10/23/06
Journal Entry:

It was early morning. As I lay in bed, I saw Jesus bring me a white horse. He urgently told me to get on the horse. So in the spirit, I did. Then I could see next to me, people all on white horses lined up for battle. Then I got a bird's eye view. The riders on white horses all advanced, in unison. Behind each of the riders were an army—like growing triangles next to each other. (It was like watching the Disney movie, The Lion, the Witch and the Wardrobe, where Peter was riding on his white horse into battle and he was leading his army like a growing triangle, into battle.) But this time, it was magnified, with many riders on many white horses, all in unison, all being followed by an army division. In the far distance, I saw the black ugly horde of the enemy. We were heading into battle.

10/30/08
Journal Entry:

I could see myself again in heaven, riding a white horse. I was riding into battle and holding tight onto the horse. I was hitting the enemy's army, yet somehow I was rising above it.

I was encountering the enemy, yet I kept feeling like I was surrounded by a hedge of protection because of the power of the Blood of Jesus.

11/3/06
Journal Entry:
Kyla gave the following word: "Be courageous in God. Look up! Look up—for the Savior of the world is here!"

Kingdom Perspective:
Every thing that can be shaken will be shaken!

6/12/09
Journal Entry:
I saw Jesus' hands. Sand was falling through His fingers. Inside His hands were structures. I saw a sand castle, sand buildings, sand homes, and sand marriages (I saw 2 sand people holding hands). Then I heard Him say, "Every thing that can be shaken will be shaken. Now is the time of the parable of foundations. What are you building on and with? Sand or rock? Sand structures are collapsing. This is the will of God. 'And the rains came down and floods came up. But the house on the sand went 'splat!' Let him who has ears, hear what I (Jesus) am saying in this hour. Time is short and judgment is coming."

As I continued to look at His hands with the sand structures, I also saw some solid structures, marriages built out of solid materials like concrete and metal. Suddenly, all the sand structures were collapsing in His hands and the sand was falling through His fingers. Then I saw His hands again. There was no more sand falling through His fingers.

When I looked at His open palms, there was a bright light shining out of it. He spoke. "This light represents the church. In the bright light, I saw solid homes, buildings, and marriages. They looked like they were built out of steel and metal. This represented solid materials. Jesus spoke again. "Do you see what I am doing in this hour? Let him who has ears, hear and listen to what I, Jesus, am saying. All that can be shaken will be shaken. All things made of sand will be exposed and crumble. Time is short. Judgment is coming and it begins with the house of the Lord."

*𝕶ingdom 𝔓erspective:
The Plumb Line

January 1ˢᵗ, 2009
Journal Entry:

As I woke up on the first day of the year and waited in silence before the Lord, this is what He spoke to my heart.

"Do you see my plumb line? It is I. It has to be all about Me or it's not of Me. It is not coincidence that you have this new journal. (On the cover is Proverbs 4:23 (NIV): Above all else, guard your heart, for it is the wellspring of life.) This is a wellspring journal and it will overflow and be a wellspring of the hidden things of My heart. WRITE! As you sit quietly and listen, I will speak and show you hidden things and then you will write . . . the book . . . your book. It will be written in this way so set aside time to listen and then to write. You are My friend and My favor rests upon you and your sister and your families."

As I looked down, I saw the words "destiny image" pop out at me. Jesus then said "Liza, it is your destiny to look and become Me, in My image. Walk into your destiny."

After He spoke, I was intrigued as to what the Lord meant by plumb line so I looked it up.

Being "plumb" is a construction term that refers to being straight up and down. A "plumb line" is a string with a weight on the end. When you hold the string at the top, the weight makes the line hang down straight. A plumb line is used especially to determine verticality.

I found "a plumb line" in Amos 7:7. *"This is what he showed me: The Lord was standing by a wall that had been built true to plumb, with a plumb line in his hand. And the LORD asked me, "What do you see, Amos?" "A plumb line," I replied. Then the Lord said, "Look, I am setting a plumb line among my people Israel; I will spare them no longer".*

Kingdom Perspective:
The Dividing Line

4/20/07
Journal Entry:
Revelations 2:11 (NIV)—"He who has an ear, let him hear what the Spirit says to the churches. He who overcomes will not be hurt at all by the second death."

The Lord spoke the following to my heart.

"The time of the Great Divide has already begun. Do not be surprised at the fiery ordeals that you are in or are about to be in. I AM WHO I AM. Trust Me. I am testing and exposing hearts and I am exposing the true nature of what lies within. Trust Me. Listen for My Voice. Rest in Me. Wisdom is being freely offered and given to those who ask for her. Ask for Wisdom. It is time to command shackles to be broken. It is time for the prisoners to be set free. I AM the Great I AM. Do not doubt. Do no fear. If you do, be quick to repent. As far as the East is from the West, I will remember your sins no more. I AM merciful, slow to anger, abounding in love and compassion. I am coming . . . . SOON! Be willing. Be waiting. Be faithful. Be true. I will honor those who honor Me."

6/29/09
Journal Entry:

As my friend and I waited on the Lord at our (former) church building, she saw a lion in the spirit, walking down the aisle from the back of the building. "Is it good or bad?" I asked. As I closed my eyes, I could see the lion too. It looked like Aslan and I then knew it was Jesus as the Lion of Judah. He stopped halfway down the aisle. "Stand up My queens." He said. So we quickly stood up. Then He opened His mouth up and roared/breathed on us. Sheesh! It was so powerful! Other things happened which I am not allowed to write at this time. But eventually as we turned, we both saw in front of us a desert.

Then I saw Him pawing the ground with his feet, all the while looking intently at the ground. We waited on the Lord as He worked. Then He hit the ground with His paw really hard. He turned and looked intently into my eyes. Then He asked me a question. "Do you think I'm good?" "Of course!" I responded. I saw such sadness in His eyes. He spoke. "There will be those who will question My goodness. Some will say, "I'm not good.""

The judgments that are coming are because of the choices of men and leaders. Not because of Me."

Finally, on the 3rd time, He lifted up both of His front legs high off the ground and then slammed it into the ground.

Then He said, "Look out. Judgment is coming to America. Every thing that can be shaken will be shaken. Everything not of Me will fall." At this point, I could see buildings crumbling down and marriages falling apart. He continued. "I am bringing the hidden things to the surface—the dross." Then He looked intently at the ground. Living Breath came out of His mouth. All of a sudden I could see a dividing line forming from the spot that He shook with His paws—right down the middle. My friend also saw the line and she also saw people. Some were on one side of the line, and some on the other. The Lord then directed us to take out our swords and declare out loud 2 things—"Victory is the Lord's" and "For the King!" When we yelled and declared, "Victory is the Lord's", all those on one side of the dividing line turned and had their eyes instantly fixed on Jesus. When "For the King" was declared, they all in unison bowed before Him. Simultaneously, the other side seemed distracted and unprepared. And they became totally bewildered and overcome with confusion when we had yelled and declared these 2 things.

Then He stood before us. My friend saw a treasure box. I then could see it too and was told to put it on the floor. So I did. Then He told me to hold out my hand. So I did. Then I saw a beautiful key—white and very tiny. She saw it as a key with a seed and white and black colors on it, attached to it. I looked closely at the key. And I saw the words "Unconditional Love" on it. He directed me to use the key to open up the box. So I did. When the treasure box opened, all I saw was bright light shining out of it. My friend also saw a mirror in it.

11/4/11
Journal Entry:

This morning as I was waiting on the Lord, I saw 2 doors. I was allowed to see behind both of them. The first door led to a path that was going up and down mountains. The second opened up to the sky. It was blue and filled with white fluffy clouds. I was then asked to choose one door. I asked the Lord which He wanted me to choose. Immediately I sensed it was to be my choice. I wanted the 2nd door because I wanted to fly. And I knew He wanted me to fly. I also sensed it represented the higher place.

Then I saw a dividing line. It was different from the 1st dividing line that I saw. I kept getting the phrase "Relentless Obedience." I was told that I needed to step over and cross this line (of relentless obedience) to get to door #2. So I crossed over the line and chose to be relentlessly obedient to the Lord so that I could fly.

*Kingdom Perspective:
*Be prepared
for what is coming*

11/29/07
Journal Entry:

If My people would learn to just seek Me. Seek Me first. Adore Me. Worship and adore Me. As they see Me, then . . . then My sweet Presence will come. And I will show Myself to them. And they shall see My glory. And even taste it.

Mighty Ones ascribe to the Lord the glory due His name. I am coming . . . soon. Be ready! Be prepared! Do not be caught in slumber or off guard for the days are evil and time is short . . . oh so short. I am coming soon.

01/13/08
Journal Entry:

1:11 or 11:11. I keep seeing the number one over and over again. Why? Please give me understanding. And please show me how/what to pray Lord. This has been a difficult time and season. It amazes me Lord that You are going to come back for a pure and spotless bride esp. when I see the dross in my own heart. Insecurities, fears, jealousy, envy, pride, selfish ambition . . . As I look at myself and at those around me, I marvel at Your amazing grace and love.

What are You teaching me this season? To love ultimately.

The ultimate question isn't whether to serve or not to serve. Rather it is to whom are you truly serving? Jesus? Yourself? Others? A cause? An organization?

Then Jesus speaks. "The heart and its hidden motives are of utmost importance to Me Liza. There is no condemnation for those who are in Me. Neither should you or anyone else in the body condemn another. Missing the mark can be by miles or millimeters—but both miss it. Liza, I will work all things out for GOOD, in all of my children, according to My purposes. Do you remember what I showed you in heaven? Hold on to that picture. Fight the good fight well to the end. I am He who is faithful and true. Trust Me. I am big enough."

Relationship and Intimacy—that's what it's all about with Jesus.

Kingdom Perspective:
Time is short
and the clock is ticking . . .

6/09/09
Journal Entry:
3:27 am—The Lord woke me up and I immediately got the following:

The clock is ticking and time is short
Does anybody hear Me knocking at the door?

You've asked Me for help
And now I've come to your door
Will you recognize Me and let Me in?
Or are you blind and unsure.

Woe to those who don't recognize Me
I'm coming in the new
It is time for the parable of the virgins to be pursued
Is your lamp lit? Do you have extra oil?
As you wait for your bridegroom?

Jesus the warrior is coming back as Lord of the Hosts
With fire in eyes, and tattoo on His thigh
Wielding His mighty sword

He's knocking and calling out your name
Do you have the ears to hear the master's voice?

The clock is ticking . . .

11/11/09
Journal Entry:

I saw Jesus holding a clock. As I looked at it, I saw it was 3 minutes to 12. There was not much time left. I got Romans 13:12.

Romans 13:12 (NASB)—"The night is almost gone, and the day is near Therefore let us lay aside the deeds of darkness and put on the armor of light."

Then He spoke. "It's time to share what's on the scrolls."

1/7/12
Journal Entry:

I was spending time with Jesus when I saw wheat—ripe and ready for harvest. I saw Jesus' hand moving over the top of the heads of wheat in the field. I could feel the urgency and concern in His heart for the harvest. "Who will harvest the wheat for Me?" He asked. And there was no clock. It was already time.

*Kingdom Perspective:
The Valley of Decision

08/2009
Journal Entry:
The Valley of Decision

I saw a person beckoning me to follow. I wasn't sure if it was an angel or Jesus. All I heard was "The Father is calling." I followed. I saw the cloud of witnesses standing and watching all in one direction. I wasn't sure if it was the same cliff over the sea that He had shown me before. As I looked in the same direction that they were looking, I saw a huge valley. It was filled with people. On the right side of the valley were paths leading down into it. People were walking down these paths. There were multitudes (seemed like millions) in it. I couldn't make out any individuals. The sense I got was that this was the valley of decision. Many of the people were leaders. And all of them were dressed in white. As individuals humbled themselves before the LORD and allowed His righteous judgments to pierce their hearts, to be transparent and fully surrendered, a bright light from above would illuminate this person and the angels would then tend to this person and lift him/her out of this valley. Sadly, many stayed where they were. They remained standing. Those that refused to judge themselves and refused to humble themselves before the LORD were then righteously judged. The ground shook tremendously. Then I saw that their eyes were blackened and their tongues were cut off. Some even had arms cut off.

After this, I wrote the following poem:

The Valley of Decision

In the Valley of Decision,
My leaders are found,
To bow ones' heart before Me
Or to stand in one's own righteous acts.

Delusion was prominent
As some were so blinded by their accomplishments and former victories.
They thought they were led here by the enemy and not by God alone.
It is not enough to start well or to run most of the race,
But end up being disqualified in the end.

Finish the race!
Run in such a way as to win the race.
And be faithful and true to the end.
By bowing one's heart in true humility, and
By allowing the dross to be exposed and burned off,
A pure heart will be produced.
And it will be one that God can entrust with His glory and
power in the final battle.

09/05/09
Journal Entry:

At Elevate, as we worshiped, I saw Dwight dressed so handsomely in his armor. Jesus was on His white horse with Dwight standing on the ground next to Him. Dwight was Jesus' servant. His position was to serve Jesus, to help hold the reins of His horse and to be near to Jesus to serve Him.

I saw my friend and I on white horses. As we responded corporately to Him in worship and as we bowed in submission and humility, I began to see horses with riders on them, climbing out of the valley of decision. It was awesome to behold. Later, I saw His army, some on white horses, some on foot, all in unison, marching forward in a straight line. Jesus was the leader and we were marching forward in perfect unity and precision with Him.

9/04/09
Journal Entry:

This morning, as I was waiting in silence before Him, I saw the Lion of Judah. He was pounding the ground with His paws. I also saw the line of decision. Then He spoke. "The time is now! Judgment begins for My people in the Valley of Decision."

11/13/09
Journal Entry:

Tonight, He gave me the following: "The time and season of My grace is soon ending. Sides must be chosen. Get off the fence and choose this day whom you will serve." Then I saw scales. "Heart motives are being weighed. Spirit Man, Rise Up! Stand Spirit Man!"

*𝕶ingdom 𝕻erspective:
Being Faithful to the End

09/22/09
Journal Entry:

As I sat in the kitchen, immediately I felt the presence of the Lord. As I waited, at first I kept getting the word "time" and was wondering if timing was what He was trying to get my attention with. Then I sensed there were others beginning to gather around me.

As I turned to my right, I saw Aimee Semple McPherson. She was wearing a white outfit. Then I noticed someone coming to my left. But I didn't know who it was. "Lord, help me. Who is it?" I asked. "It's a king." He replied. "Okay, Lord but which one?" I asked.

At first I thought with excitement "Is it King David?" But immediately I knew it wasn't. As I continued to wait, I then got the word 'Asa." "Lord, is it King Asa?" I then saw the Lord give me a "thumbs up."

As I turned to this King, my mind raced with what I knew of him. He was a righteous king but wasn't faithful to God at the end of his life. Then he began to speak. "Hello daughter of the most High God. Yes, I am King Asa. I was faithful to the Lord for most of my life but at the end, I didn't finish well. My daughter, I lived for the Lord for most of my life but what truly mattered was how I finished. Our Lord desires us to be faithful to the end and to finish this race well. I didn't. But the Lord is giving me this chance to meet you and to ask you to share my life and my mistakes with others so that they don't repeat them. Learn from my life."

At that point, I turned to Aimee and I realized why she was here too. She spoke. "Yes, I too started off well but I didn't finish well, just like King Asa. There are many leaders in your time who have been faithful, who have started well and like King Asa, lived most of their lives faithful to our King Jesus. But they need to hear this message. They need to hear the truth."

As I looked around, I could see a circle of people around me. I couldn't see their faces or were given names, but I realized they were all there because they made the same mistake. For whatever reason, they started well but all of them didn't finish well.

Aimee continued. "Liza, you have taken to heart the things I last shared with you. You have put yourself under the covering of your husband and as long as you remain in that place, you will be protected. I am praying for you, that you will be faithful to the end."

I looked to Jesus who was standing in front of me. "Child, will you be My mouthpiece? Will you speak the truth to those that I send you too?" As I looked down, I asked Jesus, "Please help me to love those that You send me to." I thought about my most recent experience in walking in this. That was so painful to my heart. "Jesus, please help me also not to disdain those who You send me to. And please give me wisdom, humility and love. Help me to be faithful to the end."

Right after this, I turned to 1 Kings 15:9-15 and 2 Chronicles 16:1-14.

1 Kings 15:9-15
"In the twentieth year of Jeroboam king of Israel, Asa began to reign over Judah, and he reigned forty-one years in Jerusalem. His mother's name was Maacah the daughter of Abishalom. And Asa did what was right in the eyes of the LORD, as David his father had done. He put away the male cult prostitutes out of the land and removed all the idols that his fathers had made. He also removed Maacah his mother from being queen mother because she had made an abominable image for Asherah. And Asa cut down her image and burned it at the brook Kidron. But the high places were not taken away. Nevertheless, the heart of Asa was wholly true to the LORD all his days. And he brought into the house of the LORD the sacred gifts of his father and his own sacred gifts, silver, and gold, and vessels."

2 Chronicles 16:1-14 (Asa's Last Years)
"In the thirty-sixth year of the reign of Asa, Baasha king of Israel went up against Judah and built Ramah, that he might permit no one to go out or come in to Asa king of Judah. Then Asa took silver and gold from the treasures of the house of the LORD and the king's house and sent them to Ben-hadad king of Syria, who lived in Damascus, saying, "There is a covenant between me and you, as there was between my father and your father. Behold, I am sending

to you silver and gold. Go, break your covenant with Baasha king of Israel, that he may withdraw from me." And Ben-hadad listened to King Asa and sent the commanders of his armies against the cities of Israel, and they conquered Ijon, Dan, Abel-maim, and all the store cities of Naphtali. And when Baasha heard of it, he stopped building Ramah and let his work cease. Then King Asa took all of Judah, and they carried away the stones of Ramah and its timber, with which Baasha had been building, and with them he built Geba and Mizpah.

At that time Hanani the seer came to Asa king of Judah and said to him, "Because you relied on the king of Syria, and did not rely on the LORD your God, the army of the king of Syria has escaped you. Were not the Ethiopians and the Libyans a huge army with very many chariots and horsemen? Yet because you relied on the LORD, he gave them into your hand. For the eyes of the LORD run to and fro throughout the whole earth, to give strong support to those whose heart is blameless toward him. You have done foolishly in this, for from now on you will have wars." Then Asa was angry with the seer and put him in the stocks in prison, for he was in a rage with him because of this. And Asa inflicted cruelties upon some of the people at the same time.

The acts of Asa, from first to last, are written in the Book of the Kings of Judah and Israel. In the thirty-ninth year of his reign Asa was diseased in his feet, and his disease became severe. Yet even in his disease he did not seek the LORD, but sought help from physicians. And Asa slept with his fathers, dying in the forty-first year of his reign."

Asa's mistake:

At the final season of his life, Asa took his eyes off the Lord. He did not rely on Him. And he didn't finish the race of his life well. Let us take King Asa's plea and warning to heart. Let's keep our eyes fixed on Jesus. And let's be faithful to the very end.

*𝕶ingdom 𝕻erspective:
Some Strategies in these Last Days

6/21/09
Journal Entry:

I saw 2 things. On one side was green grass where it was plush and beautiful (to my left). On the other side (to my right), was a desolate place—barren, rocky with dead vegetation (if any). Jesus told me to hold out my hand. I held out my hand and waited. Then I felt impressed to say, "Come Lord Jesus come." Instead of seeing Jesus come, however, I saw followers of Jesus surrounding the boundaries of this destitute land. Then they lined up side by side. I also saw Dwight, myself, & a few other city leaders as part of this circle. As we became focused on the center (I didn't see Him but sensed it was Jesus standing in the middle), we all drew closer. I thought to myself how impossible it was for this tight knit group on the boundaries to get closer without squishing each other out. But miraculously, it happened with Jesus still standing in the center. This circle of people kept pushing inwards until they were all in the center with Jesus. Then He showed me the land beneath His feet. It was now healed—both lush and green!

10/08/09
Journal Entry:

As I waited on the Lord, I could see an open door in the distance. "Look at the door." So I did. It was simple & white with a doorknob. I asked the Lord what was I suppose to do with this door. I then saw the word "Future" written on it. Then He spoke again. "There is a fine line between predestination and free choice. Look again." So I did. Suddenly the door changed. It was like it was now 2 half doors put together with a hinge in the middle and 2 doorknobs, one on the right, the other on the left. The half door on the right looked very inviting. The doorknob was shiny. The door on the left looked rather drab and a little dark. I quickly wanted to open the door but then stopped and asked the Lord for Wisdom. I saw Jesus smile and sensed He was pleased. Immediately I knew I had passed a test. Whew!

Wisdom then pointed to this unusual dual door. Suddenly, it was like the skin/surface of it was peeled off and I saw this dual door as it really was. The half door on the right was now completely black. I saw 2 words, deception and death, written on it. The other door was now beautiful and breathtaking to look at. It was covered in gold and was bright.

I didn't get to see behind the black door. I think I was kind of relieved about that. But as I chose to open the left door, I was surprised to find a precarious path up a mountain. It was the mountain of the Lord. But it was the narrow way and it led me to my King Jesus.

Then Jesus spoke. "The future is about making choices. Without My Wisdom, many will not see the true nature of the doors/choices ahead of them. It is Wisdom to inquire of the Lord. It is foolishness to trust in yourself. Do not be fooled by how things appear on the surface. Ask for My Wisdom and then you will clearly see and discern things as they really are. Then you make the best choice that will lead to Me. Many in these last days will choose the door on the right because of fear—fear of the future, fear of having lack, fear of want, fear of bad things happening to them. Insecurity always is an open door to fear. The door will look good to their eyes and they will be deceived.

On the surface, choosing Me will not always look appealing or feel good because it always means dying to self and surrendering your will to Mine. But this is the door that always leads to life and to Me.

I was now wondering about that precarious path up the mountain that was behind the beautiful door. I didn't see streams of water, peaceful meadows, and green grass and lush flowers. It sure wasn't what I expected. Jesus answered my thoughts. "The future on Earth is going to be very difficult. These are the last days. For many, darkness has already covered their homes, cities and nations. Remember, this deep darkness will cover the entire world. For those that don't choose Me but choose rather to trust in themselves or in their own idols/circumstances, as they open that black door, they will find no path to walk through this darkness. There will be no goal to reach. They will have no hope. It will be chaos. For those that choose Me, there will always be a path through this darkness, and it will always lead to Me. I am the hope of the world. And as you walk through this path, you will not be alone. Simply ask for Wisdom and I will give it to you. Wisdom will be with you on your journey. Remember My promise. I will never leave you nor forsake you. Remember."

Also this morning, I asked the Lord to show me my true condition for that day. I saw myself off my white horse. I was standing next to it. Behind me, I saw a bunch of others that were part of my company. They were all standing and waiting for me to get back on my horse and lead them. "Are you over yourself?" Jesus asked me. "Yes." I humbly responded. It was sobering to see the bigger picture. When I got so self-introspective and self absorbed, I missed it. It's not about me. It's about Jesus and His Kingdom. I got back on the horse. "Victory is the Lord's!" "For the King!"

08/02/2012
Journal Entry:

I saw a narrow path. It looked like a hiking trail up the mountain. The path looked really inviting. It was lined with shiny jewels. There were tables along the path loaded with food and things to strengthen us. As I looked off the path to the far left, I saw darkness approaching. It looked like thick black clouds. Then these covered the mountain. Yet on the path, it was miraculously totally clear! As I looked up, I could see the night sky. It was brilliant with starts and amazing. Yet right off the path, it was covered with thick, black fog. Jesus was in front of us, leading the way along the path.

*Kingdom Perspective:
A Prophetic Word about these Last Days through a Child

05/22/2008
Journal Entry:
Prophetic Word given by Kyla Kobayashi, 9 ½ yrs. old
(1:30 a.m.)

I see a picture . . . kind of cartoony. It's a tree on the center of a stage. It's beautiful and looks like someone just sprinkled sparkles all over it. It's covered with fruit and the fruit looks like it just got sprinkled with sparkles too. It's so beautiful!

(Kyla also mentioned seeing peaches, pears, and many other kinds of fruit. She said they looked so beautiful but you don't want to eat it.)

Jesus said it's the tree of life.

The fruit is to take THE gospel and to share it with others.

Some will not take the fruit.
Some will take the fruit but misuse it. And then they will produce rotten fruit.
Others will take the fruit but don't use it so it then withers and dies.
Others will take it and then go outside and give it to the birds.
Still others will take it and be faithful with it. They will produce more trees of life with more good fruit.

Some will take the fruit and then sell it for money.
Some will take the fruit but then mix their own agendas into it.
Some will reject the fruit.
Some will mock it.
Some will take the fruit and then start to falsely prophesy.

I am coming soon. And I will come as a thief in the night. No one knows the time or the day. But I know it. I am coming soon. Be prepared.

Repent you mockers of God!
Repent you Buddhists!
Repent you who worship idols!

Repent those who have taken of My fruit and have done nothing with it!
Repent those who have taken of My fruit and have misused it!
Repent!

Some will not listen or repent. They will continue to use it for selfish gain. Beware of the final judgment. When you stand before Me and say "Lord, didn't I prophesy in Your name? Didn't I do miracles in Your name?" And I will say, "I never knew you."

My hearts aches for My children who knew Me but left Me. Now they are in the hot flames of hell. Oh how my heart aches for them. I am sad for those adults and children who are in the fiery flames. They didn't prepare while they still had time. Oh how I wish they had prepared themselves. They will be separated from Me forever.

Again, I come as a thief in the night. No one knows the time or the date. I am coming soon. Be prepared.

There will be those who will be faithful with the fruit. They will plant many trees of life and will bear much fruit. And others will come and eat the fruit and they in turn will plant more good trees that will then produce more good fruit.

There will be those who also plant a bad tree that will produce rotten fruit. Others will come and eat the rotten fruit and they will produce more bad trees and more rotten fruit.

There will be those who plant a tree but don't do anything with it and the tree will wither and die.

I am coming as a thief in the night. No one knows the time or the day. And I am coming soon.

Repent you mockers of His children!
Repent you Buddhists who pray to idols!
Repent you mockers of His name!
Repent those who have misused the fruit!

Some will repent and they will go back and undo the bad and they will start to produce good trees and good fruit. Others will continue to misuse it and they will die in the fiery flames of hell forever.

I am sad for my children who don't live for me. Judgment day is coming when those that have taken of the fruit will be judged first.

Repent for I am coming as a thief in the night. No one knows the time or the day. And I am coming soon.

Be prepared. I am coming soon.

Chapter 13
A Caution and a Warning in these End Times

Acts 14: 22 (NASB)
"Through many tribulations we must enter
the kingdom of God."

Matthew 7:21-23(ESV)

"Not everyone who says to me, 'Lord, Lord,' will enter the
kingdom of heaven, but the one who does the will of my
Father who is in heaven. On that day many will say to me,
'Lord, Lord, did we not prophesy in your name, and cast out
demons in your name, and do many mighty works in your
name?' And then will I declare to them, 'I never knew you;
depart from me, you workers of lawlessness.'

*Kingdom Perspective:
**As we seek His Kingdom with all our hearts, let us be careful
not to make His Kingdom
an idol over our King Himself.**

In August of 2009, Dwight and I suddenly lost a very dear &
precious sister in Christ, who was only 25 years old. On top of
the shock and pain of walking into the ER, expecting to see her
alive and then receiving the horrible news right before I saw

her that she had just passed away, one of the most difficult parts of this whole experience was having to deal with several friends who had great intentions but who had made seeking His Kingdom priority over seeking Him.

Let me explain.

As my husband and I, along with her shocked and grief stricken husband, her mother, and another dear friend, faced her dead body in the ER, we cried out to Jesus from the depths of our heart. "God, what are you doing?!!?" "Lord, we don't understand!!" "Do you want her raised from the dead? Just tell us 'YES' and we'll pray it!!" "Jesus, what are you up to??" As we desperately sought the heart of Jesus on this matter, 3 of us in that room, including Dwight and I, were mercifully shown glimpses of her in heaven with Jesus. I saw her dressed beautifully in white standing next to Jesus and holding his hand. Our friend saw her standing before her dressed in white. Then without saying anything, she simply smiled, grabbed Jesus' hand and walked away with Him. The picture Dwight got was of our oldest son Koby's hand reaching for her hand and then telling her "Aunty, come on. Let me show you around heaven . . ."

Another close friend, as he was driving to the ER, kept crying out to Jesus, "Lord, just give me a sign and I'll speak out Your command if You want to raise her from the dead! Just tell me." But as he got there and entered that ER room, he immediately sensed in his spirit that God wasn't going to ask him to do that. And he grieved and wept.

The day after her death, Dwight and I were in the midst of contacting people from our church to tell them the difficult news. And one phone call simply angered me. As I called a brother and told him the horrible news, his first words spoken with no heartfelt compassion was "Did you pray she would be

158

raised from the dead?" As I tried to share with him what the Lord had shown me, Dwight and our other friend while in that ER room and what we sensed was on the heart of the Father in this difficult, heart breaking situation, his voice remained flat and critical. I felt like I was on trial. I shared with him that although it wasn't what we wanted (we wanted her here on Earth with us), we felt His peace and we surrendered her to Jesus. He was not convinced. And as I hung up the phone, I felt judged as if my husband and I didn't have enough faith and that we didn't hear God clearly. And I felt condemned.

By the grace of God, our spiritual dad, Papa Floyd, had just flown into town to help cover and support our friend's grieving husband, mom and us. As I shared what I just experienced to our papa, I immediately saw and felt the love and compassion of Jesus flowing from his father's heart and through his gentle eyes as He listened to me. Then he straightened himself up in the sofa he was sitting in and began to calmly explain the following analogy to me. "Liza, look here." He held up his 2 hands, both closed in fists. Shaking his left fist, he explained to me that this represented the kingdom of darkness. Then shaking his right fist, he explained that this represented the kingdom of heaven. Then he said, as he advanced his right fist towards his left fist, "The kingdom of heaven is advancing on Earth. But this", he explained, as he shook his left fist, "the kingdom of darkness is not going away just yet. For now, these 2 kingdoms are in conflict and are colliding with each other on Earth. But the kingdom of heaven won't fully be established on Earth until the return of Jesus. The kingdom of darkness will remain on Earth until He returns. Until then, this area of conflict will exist, and because of it, this world will continue to have suffering, injustice and death."

Daniel 7:22(NASB):
" . . . Until the Ancient of Days came and judgment was
passed in favor of the saints of the Highest One, and
the time arrived when the saints took possession of the
kingdom."

As I stared into my spiritual papa's eyes, I felt my spirit leap inside and my heart was lifted. For me, it was a revelatory moment. I knew papa didn't mean we wouldn't experience the fullness of Christ in and through us before His return. But rather, the kingdom of heaven wouldn't fully be established on Earth until our King returned.

Why was this analogy from my papa so revelatory and freeing to me? As I was hungry for Him & seeking hard after Jesus, I began to catch some of the fresh new teachings that were being poured out on Earth around 2005: specifically Matthew 6:10. (Praying for His kingdom to come and for His will to be done and established on Earth as it already is in heaven) This gave me such a new perspective on the Lord's prayer for which I am deeply grateful. And with all my heart, I do believe and pray that His Kingdom would come and His will would be done and established on Earth as it already is in heaven.

But what I began to observe, however, was that there was a growing number of those in our family of God who took this powerful key of truth to an unhealthy extreme. They began to push this truth to such an extent that they believed every time they chose to lay hands and pray for healing or for the dead to be raised, that it should instantly happen because they willed it and because they spoke this prayer. Their eyes were on themselves, not on Jesus. The danger came when they forgot to focus on "His will be done" and instead, simply focused on "His Kingdom come . . . on Earth as it is in Heaven."

At this point I'd like to share something I experienced through a vision.

05/09
Journal Entry:

After reading a bunch of Smith Wigglesworth's stories (and falling asleep at times), I was just not getting the whole picture. I knew he was a man of great faith. He KNEW that the same power that raised Jesus from the dead lived in him. I knew God could heal every one, every single time and yet, I thought of my mom with schizophrenia, of a friend's mom (with Alzheimer's), and other situations where some got healed and some didn't. So I cried out to Jesus, "Help me Lord—I don't get it."

Then I could see Jesus with His hand stretched out to me. "Why don't you ask him (Smith Wigglesworth) yourself?", He said with a slight giggle. "Oh no", I thought as I felt so intimidated by him. And then I could see him walking towards us. "Jesus", I said nervously. "Don't worry, I'm coming with you Liza."

I saw two big leather chairs by a fireplace. Mr. Wigglesworth sat down in one and I sat in the other. He looked at me at first with a very stern look. And I tried to sit as far to the left in my chair as I possibly could. Then I heard him laugh. As I turned, I saw his huge soft smile as he said, 'I can be quite intimidating, huh?" "Yup—you sure are intimidating", I replied. "Mr. Wigglesworth, I don't get it. I don't understand."

We talked for a while. I can't believe I didn't write it all down soon after. But what I got to do was watch him as he ministered.

I watched as Mr. Wigglesworth prayed for someone. The whole time he was praying, his eyes were fixed on Jesus. And as he looked at Jesus, he intently watched Jesus' hands. He didn't act until he saw Jesus give him the hand signal to go forward. When he saw Jesus give him the signal to proceed, then he laid hands and prayed for this individual. And that person got healed. I saw him do this several times, again always with His eyes fixed intently on Jesus.

What an amazing man of God! Mr. Wigglesworth knew the truth that the same power that raised Jesus from the dead lived in him. But he never abused that power. He only did what the Father willed on Earth. What an amazing example!

Dear family of God, we can leave out His will if our eyes stray off of Jesus. There is a danger when we become unaligned and something that God meant for good becomes more important than seeking God and His will. His ways and thoughts are so much higher than ours. Yes, His desire is to ultimately heal hearts and bring souls to Himself. But sometimes, He allows delays. And sometimes, although I don't always understand why, He allows (not causes) suffering and even death, like in the case of my dear friend who passed away at 25 years old. We will not always understand.

When He does lead us to pray, we need to be obedient, and not have the fear of man. We need to be bold and to pray in faith but we need to be sure our eyes and hearts are always on Jesus. If Jesus no longer becomes our ultimate focus, we will become unaligned and off centered. And in those times, when our flesh and pride can blind us, we can run ahead of God. Like Abraham who ran ahead of God and took things into his own hands, we can birth Ishmaels. And tragically, we can have totally wrong motives when we pray, erroneously blind to the selfish ambition and pride in our own hearts as we seek awesome God things like the supernatural, including signs and wonders. If we push forward in our flesh, trying to establish His Kingdom on Earth in our own strength or for our own selfish motives—especially to draw attention to ourselves because it makes us feel important and to build our own kingdoms on Earth, we are in danger of becoming those that He mentions in Matthew 11:21-23. That's scary and dangerous!

How then should we deal with these things? We don't want to proceed in a spirit of fear, but we do want to have the fear of God and the love of the Lord as we move forward. Let's take a look at Jesus.

In Matthew 4:23, it says "*And he went throughout all Galilee, teaching in their synagogues and proclaiming the gospel of the kingdom and healing every disease and every affliction among the people.*" Then in Matthew 8:15, Jesus is at Peter's home and in verse 16 it says "*That evening, they brought to him many who were oppressed by demons, and he cast out the spirits with a word and healed all who were sick.*" And again in Matthew 9:35—"*And Jesus went throughout all the cities and villages, teaching in their synagogues and proclaiming the gospel of the kingdom and healing every disease and every affliction.*" Jesus is our role model and example. And the same power that was in Him while on Earth is now in us. (Ephesians 1) We have the same power to heal every disease and every affliction that comes our way.

But then, Jesus does a strange thing when He is in Jerusalem. In John 5: 1-17, Jesus comes to Jerusalem and is now by the Sheep Gate and the pool of Bethesda. In this place are multitudes of invalids—blind, lame and paralyzed. This sounds like a gold mine to show off the glory of God! But as Jesus walks through this place, He singles out one man, not 2, or 10 or even the entire multitude. He asks him "Do you want to be healed?" Then He says to him "Get up take up your bed and walk." And this man does. Then Jesus, in verse 13, withdraws to another place. That's it. Nothing more. Nothing less. And in this way, Jesus models to us beautifully of what it looks like to truly seek the Kingdom of God first. He simply walked in an intimate relationship with His Father in heaven and all He wanted was to do the will of His Father on Earth, being at the right place at the right time, and doing only what the Father told Him to do at that moment. In John 5:30, Jesus says *"I seek not my own will but the will of him who sent me."* This is what should always be at the center of our heart motives, especially as we move into the supernatural.

Dear family of God, it is wisdom to inquire of the Lord. We should never prioritize what God can do over who He is. It is wisdom to inquire of the Lord as to what the Father is doing at that moment—again, especially in the area of the supernatural.

Now it may be the Father's will to place you in a town and reveal to you that it's His will for every single person in that place to be healed. And if that's so and He's made that clear to you, then be obedient, step out in humility with love and pray in faith. But it may be a situation like the pool in Bethesda, that despite having a multitude of invalids-blind, lame and paralyzed, that He may want you to approach a single person and be his conduit to demonstrate His power on Earth by healing him/her. The key is to walk intimately with the Lord, to hear His voice clearly and to wisely inquire what is the Father's will in each and every situation that we face.

Going back to that difficult situation with that brother, by the grace of God, I was able to talk to him about our phone conversation. As I shared my heart with him, he humbly apologized as he realized his lack of love and compassion in this situation. I'm not sure if he also realized his act of unrighteous judgment. But I have forgiven him and we are dear friends to this day. But again, there's a valuable lesson to be learned from this.

In the ensuing week after our friend's death, we had a few folks from the Body of Christ who called my husband and I at home, still pushing what Jesus could do over who He was and what His will was in this difficult situation. I know a large part of this was because they were struggling with the shock of her unexpected death and they were understandably having a hard time dealing with it. But even after we shared what the Lord had shown us, including those visions, and also the miraculous peace of God that we were experiencing amidst this terrible loss, they continued to call to try to get the chance to pray over her dead body in the morgue. Finally, one of these friends confessed that they needed to go to the hospital in hopes of getting to pray over her dead body more for themselves than for our deceased friend's husband, mom or us. At that point, I was deeply grateful for my friend's honesty. I love this person dearly and we too are friends to this day. But I could see that this situation didn't fit my friend's perspective of what seeking His Kingdom on Earth looked like.

I love a song that Brian Johnson and John Mohr wrote. (www.bethelmusic.com) It is entitled "Where You go I'll go" (copyright 2005 Brian Johnson), and the message it conveys is powerful. In this song, the chorus states, "Where You go, I go; what You say, I say; what You pray, I pray." It makes the point that Jesus ONLY did what HIs Father asked Him to do and in that context, He ONLY said what the Father asked him to say. Furthermore, it truthfully proclaims that Jesus ONLY moved when He felt the Holy Spirit leading Him and that every move He made was in total surrender to

His Father. John 6:38 (NIV) says, *"For I have come down from heaven not to do my will but to do the will of him who sent me."* If this is how Jesus lived while on Earth and His heart was so in love and in tune with His Father, isn't this the example that we need to follow? *Jesus, please help us to love our Heavenly Father just like You. Holy Spirit, please change our hearts so that we will love HIM to the point that we will follow and seek to only live the Father's will on Earth... just like Jesus. Amen.*

———

This is wisdom.

**Kingdom Perspective:*
Caution and Warning-
So what's your heart motive?

Heart motives means everything to Jesus. And it is vital that we keep our heart and ourselves honest and right before Him.

I remember years ago, when my husband and I sat with a man who shared with us his pursuit of the supernatural. He was very dear to us and was also one of the most gifted people that we had ever met in the area of signs and wonders. When we first met him, we were in awe of his hot pursuit for the supernatural and of the testimonies of signs and wonders that he saw God do in and through him. Pretty amazing stuff!

As we spent more time with him, however, we began to see some red flags. As he shared stories with us of how he and a bunch of his friends were pursuing God in the supernatural and were fearlessly praying over the sick, our hearts began to be troubled when it became increasing clear that heart motives were not pure and that his character had some serious areas of weakness. As he began to proudly share how he and his friends stormed the ER rooms in local hospitals in his city looking for places to seek signs and wonders, he laughed smugly as he shared how those hospitals had now banned Christians from coming into their ER rooms. As we listened, however, we became increasingly concerned and saddened for this younger brother.

He also shared with us that among his kingdom seeking friends, all of them were vying to be the first among their group to raise someone from the dead. Again our hearts were troubled when we heard this, not because we didn't want the dead raised, but because it became increasing clear that the heart motives behind seeking these things had pride and selfish ambition mixed in with a lot of wonderful youthful zeal. Also, because of our own experiences with death in an ER room, we thought about the families of loved ones who had just died, being in shock and deep grief as they looked at the dead body of their loved one and then having someone from this group of unaligned kingdom seekers, coming into their ER room, pushing to lay hands on their loved one to try to raise them from the dead—because in all honesty, their heart motives were probably rooted in selfish ambition and pride.

Please hear my heart as explain. I am all for praying for the sick and for signs and wonders, as His spirit leads us. I just heard an amazing story from an intercessor in our city. This young woman was part of a DTS team from YWAM. As she and her team prayed and listened to the Lord for His directions, they heard Him clearly direct them to go to the nearest ER room. So they obeyed. When she got there, the Lord directed her to sit next a young woman. And what ensued was a divine conversation. The Lord used her to speak life and renew hope into this young woman's life. She gave all the glory to the Lord and He was totally glorified. Praise the Lord! I am also looking forward to the day when entire hospitals will clear because warriors of the Lord, led by His Spirit, love and humility, with their eyes totally fixed on Jesus, will walk into these places with boldness and faith and everyone will be healed. I know this is going to happen and I can't wait to see it happen.

But sometimes zealous, passionate people, desiring to see God's kingdom established on Earth, can run ahead of God and His leading without wisdom and humility. Zeal without these things is dangerous. I also thought about the ER workers at that hospital who were still lost without salvation and wondered what they thought of Christians now after meeting those that were blinded by selfish ambition and pride. I do pray for the day when every single ER in our city, state and nation would run to Christians, begging them to come and pray for the sick, because they see the love of Jesus, His humility and His power overflowing through us.

At this point, I'd like to share the following excerpt on one of my heroes of the faith who walked in tremendous power and authority, especially in the area of signs and wonders, John G. Lake.

In the book, <u>John G. Lake—The Complete Collection of His Life Teachings,</u> compiled by Roberts Liardon, copyright 1999, his grandson, John Lake III, wrote the following in the forward.

"Grandfather had the power of God is his life because he was utterly consumed with the prize: A closer walk with Jesus Christ and a better, clearer, more personal understanding of the nature of God and the purpose of man's journey through this world. The reward for his focus on the prize was the gift of healing he operated in so strongly. As he remained single-minded toward the goal of eliminating the barriers between the physical and spiritual realms, the power came to him, though it never took over as his focus. Grandfather was not overawed by the power to heal. It was a good gift, but his life goal was still not healing. His goal was still a closer walk with God . . . My grandfather's life was dedicated to finding the will of God and fulfilling it wholly.

Much of Grandfather's power came from simply being where God wanted him at the time God wanted him to be there."

May we have a pure heart like John G. Lake that was focused on the ultimate goal—Jesus! Let us consistently give the Holy Spirit permission to reveal any pride and selfish ambition in our hearts our hearts. May we cry out to our Lord Psalm 139: 23-24 (NLT):

"Search me, O God, and know my heart! Try me and know my thoughts! And see if there be any grievous way in me, and lead me in the way everlasting!"

May I ask you an honest question? What really is your heart's true motive? And why are you seeking the supernatural? Is it really for Jesus and for His glory alone? Or is it honestly and truthfully all about you?

If our heart is to seek the kingdom of God, including signs, wonders and the supernatural, just for our own human fleshly satisfaction and simply to fuel our pride, and we're not being rooted and grounded in deep love, intimacy and in step with Jesus and our Father in heaven, we are in deep danger of becoming those that are talked about in Matthew 7:21-23.

"Not everyone who says to me, 'Lord, Lord,' will enter the kingdom of heaven, but the one who does the will of my

Father who is in heaven. On that day many will say to me,
'Lord, Lord, did we not prophesy in your name, and cast out
demons in your name, and do many mighty works in your
name?' And then will I declare to them, 'I never knew you;
depart from me, you workers of lawlessness.'

These verses increase the fear of God in me. These people were doing kingdom things—healing, prophesying, casting out demons, and doing mighty works in Jesus' name. And yes, they were seeking to bring His Kingdom on Earth as it already is in Heaven. But who were the ones allowed to enter the kingdom of heaven? In this context, it was only the ones who did the will of the Father; therefore it is wisdom to inquire of the Father and to do only His will—not our own. It even says in these verses that "On that day <u>MANY</u> will say to me, Lord, Lord, did we not prophesy in your name . . . and do many mighty works in your name?" That's heavy! It's not a few, several, or some—but many. And Jesus is going to declare to them, "*I never knew you; depart from me, you workers of lawlessness.*"

If we prioritize and push His kingdom on Earth—in our own flesh—and we aren't in tune with the Father's heart, we will do much damage and cause much hurt, both in the body of Christ and in the lost. And horribly, we may miss being allowed to enter His kingdom. That is tragic. It is wisdom to inquire of the Lord. And it is important that our heart is right and pure before Him.

One of the last conversations I had with this young man was about this topic. We talked about heart motives and about some of the red flags that my husband and I had witnessed in his life. It was a tough and difficult conversation. At the very end, he shared that he felt our church family wasn't seeing signs and wonders like he was and he strongly felt we were missing it. I shared with him that we were going to seek Jesus first and that these things were going to follow in His timing. He strongly disagreed and said he was going to seek the signs and wonders. I told him we were going to seek Jesus. So we had to agree to disagree and we had to part ways. My husband and I still love him deeply. I pray Jesus would truly be in the center of his heart and that the Lord would continue to bring revelation to those areas that aren't aligned to the cross.

*Kingdom Perspective:
Caution and warning-
Beware of pride and disdain

03/08/09
Journal Entry:

As I walked into a store with my husband and children, I noticed an individual that I had met briefly at a citywide leadership meeting. Immediately I heard the Lord speak. "Liza, watch carefully. I have an important lesson that I want you to learn." My husband and 2 children went ahead while my oldest paused with me. Not knowing why I had stopped, she simply took this moment to wrap her arms around my waist and give me a big, long hug. And as I wrapped my arms around my daughter and held her for awhile, I watched with interest as I saw this person march to the cash register with a face set with irritation and resoluteness to the 2 store clerks waiting there.

Without any introduction or politeness, this individual curtly retorted to the store clerk the following statement. "I haven't found anything in this store that I like. Don't you have a policy about this? So what are you going to do about it? What are you going to give me to compensate for this?" I was inwardly shocked at the brazenness of what was just demanded as I saw the store clerk's eyes widen as she was taken aback by this crisp comment and demand. I watched as this person demanded compensation as the poor store clerk tried to offer discount coupons to appease this individual. And as I observed all of this, I felt the sorrow and anger of God.

You see, when I met this person at this leadership meeting of pastors, the title this individual used as an introduction was "Apostle so and so." This person was new to our city and it was the first time most of us had met this individual. And as I continued to discretely watch this scene, the Lord spoke to my heart.

"Liza, in these last days, I am raising up true apostles who will walk in true humility and love. Do you see the importance of this lesson I'm trying to teach you tonight? Can you imagine if this individual who claims to be my apostle holds a meeting in your city and these 2 store clerks happened to show up. What will they think of this person's message after what just happened? And what will they think of Me? Can you see the importance of godly character overflowing with the fruit of my Spirit? Can you see why humility versus pride and self-righteousness is so vital? I desire the lost to find Me as they see Me in you."

I felt sadness and the fear of the Lord as I thought about this person possibly standing before the throne of God at the end of time and facing His judgment. And I thought back to my past, and those times that I got puffed up in my own value or position and had treated others disdainfully or with no love, patience or compassion. And I repented. As I walked away from this scene to my husband and children, I cried out to the Lord from my heart. "Jesus, please keep me humble! Help me face Your judgments now on Earth before I stand before

Your throne as You go over my life. And help me to love." And again, the Lord spoke to my heart. "The true apostles and prophets that I am raising up in these last days won't flaunt their titles before others or even use them in these last days. They will be marked by deep humility and will come to serve others with love. My authority will be evident to all for they will move in great power and wisdom." After He finished speaking, I cried out to Him. "Please give me wisdom, love & humility and please help me never to forget the lessons of this night. Thank you Lord. I am deeply grateful to You for showing me this tonight. Amen."

I also remember having lunch with some friends that flowed in the supernatural. I love them each dearly. But as we were eating, we started to discuss a man who had lost his vision and was now blind. He was given the opportunity to have his eyesight fully restored through surgery but chose to remain blind because he felt it was a gift from God that allowed him to relate to people with his other senses in such a more powerful way in his profession.

I remember feeling literally hit in the stomach when all of a sudden, they began to judge this man, saying that he was full of fear, that this wasn't God's will or heart for him and that he was wrong in choosing to remain blind. I remember looking into their eyes as I thought to myself, "You guys have never met this man. I have. I have heard him share his testimony and have seen the powerful fruit of his life and ministry. You guys haven't. And if he does have some hidden fear, shouldn't you have gentleness and compassion towards him and not presumptuously judge and disdain him?" I looked at my other friend, who had also personally met and heard this man's testimony and I could see the look of shock and sadness in her eyes that reflected what I felt in my heart.

As I sat there appalled, I continued to listen to my friends talk about God's kingdom to an extreme. And I watched as I saw what the knowledge of truth could do to people. It can puff you up. What I sensed and saw was that there was no love or gentleness towards this man, just unrighteous judgment. I love these friends. I tried to share about this man and about his life and testimony with them. But at that point, they were utterly convinced they were right. So I just stopped speaking, realizing we were just going to have to disagree on this one. But as I looked at the fruit and saw the lack of love or humility, I was so saddened. Wisdom is to first ask the Father "How do You see this man? What do You say about this situation? Please give me your heart, your eyes, your love and your will for this fellow brother in this situation." If Papa God tells us that this man did fall short, then our heart response should be filled with compassion & humility. And with love, we need to pray that the Lord out of His mercy would reveal this to him and give him true revelation of his spiritual condition. **We can be right, but if there's no love, we've missed the point.**

Our Lord is merciful and compassionate. This chapter was not an easy one for me to write but I wrote it out of obedience. Please know that if this chapter has convicted you, it is because of His goodness and love that He's allowed your spirit to be convicted of any sin, weakness or area that has become unaligned. He loves you. He never condemns. He only convicts. And He is interceding for you at the right hand of the Father. His desire is that we know the truth so that we can be set free. It is our freedom that He is really after because He knows that when we're truly free, we will get to experience the fullness of His glory in and through us on Earth as it already is in Heaven.

I want to end this chapter with 2 journal entries of times when I struggled with my weaknesses and sin. I pray it would encourage your heart.

03/02/09
Journal Entry:

These past 10 days have been tough as I felt the battle of doubt and unbelief versus believing God as you revealed more of the calling on my life. I also felt the battle of pride/false humility versus true humility raging in my mind and heart.

Faith and trust, that's an issue for me. As I whined and focused my eyes on myself, I saw You standing nearby. You remained so patient and steadfast with me as I continued to wallow in self-pity and condemnation. Then I saw a picture of myself about the age of Kailee (4), crying and whining about myself as You, as my parent, were just waiting for me to get over myself and then move on.

Then another night, as I mentally beat myself up and felt tormented as I struggled with double mindedness in my mind, I cried out to You. In response, You gave me a huge bowl. I asked You (Jesus) what it was. You said it was a bowl filled with the prayers of the saints. They were praying for me.

Then this morning, again I felt beaten up and discouraged. As I cried out to You and waited, I immediately sensed You were in the room. I then could see You (Jesus) standing in front of me with leaders from the cloud of witnesses next to you. I cried out, "Does anybody else struggle with this like me?" Immediately I could feel the love and empathy from these leaders. Each of them had faced the same struggles while on

Earth. Some of them didn't win this battle while on Earth and at the end of their lives, gave in to pride. But I felt such love.

They were all praying and interceding for me because they understood the struggles of a leader—to remain humble of heart and to keep Jesus on the throne of his/her heart. Thank you Jesus that You love me as I am. And thank you for those that have gone before me and who are praying and interceding for me. I am blessed.

08/29/10
Journal Entry:

This morning, I was still struggling, repenting and crying out to the Lord. Then I got the following vision: I saw a tunnel that I was traveling down. All of a sudden, instead of traveling forward, I made a sharp turn and began spinning in a circle going nowhere. I was deeply convicted! And this made me desperate for God. I cried out to the Lord to help me guard my heart and to help my unbelief. All of a sudden, I saw myself on my horse. He said, "Come." So I did. I found myself on my horse in front of a river. "Jump in", He said. So I did. And as I did, I immediately felt the water cleanse me from all impurities. It was His river of life. I then heard, "Restored." This reverberated in my spirit! I was restored by His grace.

As further proof, He then handed me a mirror. As I looked in the mirror, I looked at my heart and body. I was amazed to see that I was totally clean and whole. I was reminded of that verse that says, "His mercies are new every morning." I was deeply grateful for His mercy and grace. Lord, help me to extend that same grace to others. Help me to be steadfast and immovable. Thank you Jesus!

Chapter 14
Seeking His Kingdom AND His Righteousness

Matthew 6:33(ESV)—"But seek first the kingdom of God <u>and</u> his righteousness, and all these things will be added to you."

In this verse, Jesus admonishes us that we need to seek first the kingdom of God **AND** his righteousness. Sometimes we forget the 2nd part. And when we forget to also seek His righteousness while we're seeking His kingdom, we become unaligned. The word righteousness in this verse comes from the Greek word "Dikaiosune" (dik-ah-yos-oo'-nay). This word is defined as "being in a state of him who is as he ought to be, righteousness, the condition acceptable to God and includes having integrity, virtue, purity of life, rightness, correctness of thinking feeling, and acting." When we seek His righteousness, we're seeking to be just like Jesus—having the right heart, the right attitudes, the right motives, the right way of thinking of feeling and acting, especially towards others. That's why it is so vital that as we seek His kingdom with all our hearts, we are also just as vigilantly seeking His righteousness.

There is a growing generation of followers of Jesus who are seeing the horrible injustices in our world and who want to feed the hungry, and be Jesus. But some of them are also seeing the extreme abuses of those that are pushing His Kingdom from impure hearts, and are having a growing distaste towards those they view as "thrill seekers" or "selfish" who they've discerned as only wanting to seek the supernatural, signs and wonders for their own selfish gain-without impacting the hurting world.

It is true that some of them may push away from the supernatural because of fear or because of some deep wounds that were inflicted upon them from those that abused God's supernatural power. But there are those in this camp who are simply discerning when they see selfishness along with self-righteous pride and/or unrighteous judgment mixed with the pushing of God's kingdom on Earth. And this makes some in our Body of Christ irritated or even angry. Sadly, some of these brethren have responded by pushing away from the supernatural facet of Jesus and from the moving of His Spirit through spiritual gifts.

There are also those in the body of Christ who are afraid to move forward in seeing His Kingdom established on this Earth because of the fear of man. When they sense the Holy Spirit telling them to be bold and to offer prayer for someone to be healed, they respond in fear of being possibly rejected or of not having this person healed if they pray. So they hold back. This is something the Lord desires to breakthrough and release healing, courage, faith, revelation of His perfect love that casts off all fear, boldness and so on.

To help bring understanding and discernment to this situation, let me share the following analogy that my husband Dwight shared with me:

Pursuing Jesus is like climbing up a steep mountain. On one side is the fear of man. At the top of the mountain is Jesus. And on the other side is the disdain of man. Both sides of the mountain lack true love. To stay at the top requires us to keep our eyes on Jesus and to love.

Matthew 12:25 (ESV) says, *"Every kingdom divided against itself is laid waste, and no city or house divided against itself will stand."* As the family of God, we need to stop being divided. Love covers a multitude of sins. Mercy triumphs over judgment. When we see the extremes, we need to respond with humility and prayer. When the Lord gives us revelatory insight, wisdom, and favor, we need to walk in humble mercy and grace with those that may not see as we do. And we need to not disdain them. A verse the Lord gave me regarding this was Romans 15:1 (ESV): *"We who are strong have an obligation to bear with the failings of the weak, and not to please ourselves."* We need to seek Jesus, in all His fullness and facets. And we need to love.

Rick Joyner, in his book, The Apostolic Ministry, says the following:

"In the first century, Christianity was a super-natural experience. God is supernatural. If we are going to experience God, it will be a supernatural experience. If we are going to walk with God, we must become comfortable with the supernatural. In the early church the Lord Himself appeared to people at times. There were interchanges with angels to the degree that the church was exhorted to be careful how they treated strangers, because they could be angels. The Lord was very close to His people, and the spiritual realm was very familiar to all believers. This made it easier for them to endure the almost continual opposition, persecution and afflictions."

I believe we need to fully embrace the supernatural because we serve a supernatural God. And we need to embrace all of Jesus. Likewise, I also believe we need to prepare ourselves for an increase of opposition, persecution, suffering and affliction. The darkness is going to increase. But so is the light of His glory. And we need to be the light of the world. We need to lead the way in feeding the hungry and helping the homeless and we need to be Jesus beyond the walls of our church buildings.

And dear Family of God—we need to get along. We need to stop passing unrighteous judgment on one another. We need to be quick to forgive each other and to love unconditionally. I confess that I've been part of the extreme that chased hard after the supernatural, pushing His kingdom on Earth as it is in heaven and then have looked upon fellow brothers and sisters who weren't as hungry for signs and wonders or who weren't chasing after the supernatural as hard as myself with impatience, self righteous pride, and disdain. Likewise, I've been part of those that strongly fought for social justice and for helping the poor and needy and have looked at those chasing hard after the supernatural with the same disdain, unrighteous judgment and even unrighteous fear, especially when I discerned selfish ambition and pride. I've also struggled (and still honestly do a times) with the fear of man. I've been at both extremes, and at both sides of the mountain of the Lord. And I've had to humble myself before Jesus and repent. Dear family, we all need to do the same.

Let's start with judging our own hearts first. Do we look down on other brothers and sisters who aren't chasing the same things we are? Are we pushy and arrogant? Or are we known as lovers of Jesus and peacemakers in His kingdom. If you are hungry for Jesus, be grateful with a humble heart. He placed that hunger inside of you. And then with love and true humility, pray for those that aren't as hungry for Him—that He would stir up hunger inside of them. Do not judge unrighteously. If you're not sure, check your heart. Do you have love and the fruit of the spirit? Or is pride and impatience at the root of your response?

For those that are seeking to see social injustices righted and who are totally into feeding the homeless and being the hands and feet of Jesus, how do you look at those that are focused mainly on seeking the supernatural? Freaks? Weirdoes? Selfish thrill seekers who don't give a rip about a lost and dying world? How do you respond when they manifest supernatural things, like shaking or falling out under the spirit? Do you have the fear of man? Is your first question "What will people think?" Or is your first question "What do You think? Is this of You?" If you're not sure, look at the fruit.

Matthew 7:1-2 (ESV):
"Judge not, that you be not judged. For with the judgment you pronounce you will be judged, and with the measure you use it will be measured to you."

1 Peter 4:8 (ESV):
"Above all, keep loving one another earnestly, since love covers a multitude of sins."

I pray that we will do this dear family of God. On pg. 378-379 of the book, <u>John G. Lake—The Complete Collection of His Life Teachings</u>, John G. Lake himself wrote the following passage:

"The greatest manifestation of the Holy Ghost-baptized life ever given to the world was not in the preaching of the apostles; it was not in the wonderful manifestation of God that took place at their hands. It was in the **UNSELFISHNESS** manifested by the Church. Think of it. Three thousand Holy ghost baptized Christians in Jerusalem from the Day of Pentecost onward, who love their neighbor's children

181

as much as their own, who were so anxious for fear their brethren did not have enough to eat that they sold their estate and brought the money and laid it at the apostle's feet. They said, "Distribute it, carry the glow and the fire and the wonder of this divine salvation to the whole world." That showed what God had wrought in their hearts. Oh, I wish we could arrive at that place, where this church was baptized in that degree of unselfishness. That would be a greater manifestation than healing, greater than conversion, greater than baptism in the Holy Ghost, greater than tongues. It would be a manifestation of the **LOVE** of 1 Corinthians 13 that so many preach about and do not possess."

May we gleam all that God desires us to gain through this godly man's pure heart.

Jesus prayed the following for us in John 17:25-26 (ESV). *"O righteous Father, even though the world does not know you, I know you, and these know that you have sent me. I made known to them your name, and I will continue to make it known, that the love with which you have loved me may be in them, and I in them."*

*Kingdom Perspective:
True unity is NOT uniformity.
It is embracing our uniqueness and diversity that the Lord has created in us.

I remember a meeting I was at because a group needed to use our church building and sound system. As I sat in the room listening to the guest speaker and his wife, I began to really struggle being there. I began to pick up people's spiritual baggage and I was becoming increasingly irritated at the flamboyant style of the speaker. A trusted friend & intercessor from another church was there with me and she shared a vision that the Lord gave to her that confirmed to me that not all was rightly aligned.

As I went home, I had to repent of having a condescending attitude towards this out of town guest speaker. I found my flesh rising up in pride as I saw the rotten fruit of self-righteousness beginning to appear in my heart. Pride is such a horrible thing. As I repented, I asked the Lord to show me what He saw. This is what He showed me:

I saw a picture of a slice of strawberry cream cheese pie. He said this slice represented Elevate and me. Then I saw lots of different slices of desserts: chocolate dobash, peach Bavarian, custard pie, German chocolate, and so on. These represented other churches & other movements. At first, when I saw all these slices, I wondered how they would all fit and come together as a whole. Jesus told me that this wasn't the focus of this analogy.

Next, I saw the lost and other people eating various types of desserts depending on their likes and dislikes. Then Jesus spoke. He said that some people that came last night to the meeting only liked this style. I didn't like it. Others like me preferred other desserts (styles) better. All these slices were good and important to Him. Ultimately, His purpose behind providing all these varieties of desserts (styles) was for the lost to come to Him. Then Jesus gently but firmly told me the following: "You must love and not disdain or unrighteously judge other people, movements and churches. Likewise, they need to learn to do the same."

As my heart pondered these things, I was reminded of 1 Peter 4:8 (NIV). "*Above all, love each other deeply because love covers a multitude of sins.*" Yes, things weren't totally aligned that night but the Lord reminded me that I wasn't perfect either. And the main source of my irritation was simply the speaker's style. So I prayed a simple prayer: "Lord, help me to recognize You in others, regardless of their different style or flavor. Help me to embrace diversity in the body of Christ. Help me to love. In Your Name, amen."

Rick Joyner, in the his book, The Call, wrote the following:

"We were created different for a reason. True peace will only come when we respect the distinctions we have. When we really know who we are, we will never be threatened by those who are different. When we are free, we are free to show those who are different from us honor and respect, always seeking to learn from one another, just as you are now doing with me. (pg. 106)

03/07/08
Journal Entry:

True Unity—What does that look like? Walk by the Spirit and you will not carry out the desires of the flesh. True unity happens when we totally submit to the leading of the Holy Spirit. As we submit to Him, we then submit to one another in love. John 17:21 (ESV)—*"That they may all be one, just as you, Father, are in me, and I in you, that they also may be in us, so that the world may believe that you have sent me."*

Problems happen, when in our quest to submit to the leading of the Holy Spirit, we allow presumptuousness to come in. We then add in our own human understanding of what true freedom should look like.

True freedom in Christ looks different for everyone. For all, it does entail getting over the fear of man and obeying the prompting of the Holy Spirit to say and do whatever He wants in His timing and direction, but always with love. But for one, it's to yell. For another, it's to dance. For another, it's to fall on their face and groan. For yet another, it's to laugh in the spirit. And for another, it's to be silent in deep reverence in His presence. True freedom and unity is covered by love and the grace to give each other the freedom to move as the Holy Spirit directs.

10/03/08
Journal Entry:

I saw a chessboard with chess pieces on it. I saw a hand. It was a nail pierced hand so I knew it was Jesus. His hand was moving the pieces into place on the board. The pieces were all different shapes. Some were battered more than others. Other pieces were brand new and made out of very shiny polished metal. Other pieces looked really old and antique. These pieces were all different but every one of them had a use and a purpose. I sensed these pieces represented movements of God. No one movement had it all. Then I heard Jesus say, "I am giving every single piece something unique."

As I thought about this chessboard and these unique pieces, I was convicted of those times I had unrighteously judged and written off some of these old movements. I had taken pride in how our piece looked, rather new and shiny. And I realized that Jesus loved every one of these equally and He had an end time purpose for each one. And again I was reminded of the importance of love.

Then the Lord gave me the following word:

"I am assembling an army of mighty ones. Do you see them? Do you remember when I summoned you to call them from the East, the West, the North and the South? That was My call, My will. And they are now coming. Do you see them? I've raised you and Dwight together to help lead and shepherd these mighty ones for now, for a season.

Child, more are coming. I am bringing them. They need to be sent out with My (the Father's) blessing. Embrace them, love them, encourage them, believe them in their individual callings and destinies.

Do not fear. Each of them that come will bring a flavor, a (spirit) spice. I am cooking a broth that is out of this world. Taste and see that the Lord is good! This will become a signature, a mark of your church. Continue to seek Me. I AM big enough. I AM able to do this thing. And I AM will do it!"

11/17/11
Journal Entry:

I saw Jesus' hands conducting us. Each of us had our eyes glued to his hands and his conducting stick. On cue, we would each play our part; each on his/her own unique instrument, making beautiful music.

My prayer:

Lord, please establish in Your church, a culture of honor and of love. Help us to recognize the beauty in our unique, God given differences. Lord, help Your children to take root downward and bear fruit upward. As we love and keep our eyes focused on You alone, may You make us one in true unity that the world may believe in Jesus.

2 Kings 19:30, 31b (ESV)
*"And the surviving remnant of the house of Judah shall
again take root downward and bear fruit upward. The zeal
of the LORD will do this."*

Chapter 15
It will cost us everything . . .

4/8/06
Journal Entry:

It was time for bed. I put Kailee down in her crib for the night and it was just Kairos and I left in the living room. The song "God of Wonders" was playing and I stood and raised my hands in worship. Kairos (now 4 years old) sat in the recliner and lifted his hands in worship as well. I felt led to lay my hands on his head and pray for him. I could really feel the presence and anointing of God.

Later, as Dwight and I went to pray with Kairos and Kyla in their bedroom, I found him lying in his bed very quiet and not in his normal sleeping position. "Kairos, are you okay?" I asked. He looked very quiet and sober. "Are you sad?" "No mommy, I'm okay," he replied. "Are you tired?" "No mommy, I'm okay." Then Kairos began to speak. "Mommy, I die for God." My heart raced as the words "What?" fell from my lips. "What did you say? 'Mommy, I die for God?'" At that point, my oldest daughter Kyla rolled over in the bunk bed. She was shocked as she asked point blank "Kairos, did you say die?" Dwight, seeing the situation, quickly diverted Kyla's attention to her fish tank in the room. I turned my attention back to Kairos.

"Son, what did you say? I do? I did for God?" "Mommy . . ." he said as he looked up at me with calmness in his voice and spirit. "No, mommy. I die for God." Tears pooled in my eyes and started to flow down my cheeks as my heart ached. I lost it. I held my breath and felt like I could barely see or breathe because I didn't want to sob uncontrollably in front of my son. Kairos then moved to his regular position in his bed. I crawled over to where he was lying, as the tears continued to freely flow from my eyes. Then I faced him and gently caressed his face. "Son, you belong to Jesus." Kairos looked up at me and peaceably nodded. "If Jesus wants you to die for him. So be it." As I spoke those words out loud, my heart cried out "Lord, He is not mine but Yours! He belongs to You. Let it be done to him according to Your will." After my heart spoke that last line, I just started to quietly sob as my eyes remained closed. Suddenly, I felt Kairos' little hands gently caressing my face. I looked down and our eyes locked. "Mommy, it's okay. It's all right. I be here for awhile." I sobbed louder. His hand continued to brush my cheek and caress my face. "Mommy, it's okay. It's all right." I smiled down at him and kissed him goodnight as I buried my face into his little chest. He held me tight. "I love you Mommy." Then he grabbed my face and kissed me on my lips. I bathed his face with my tears. Then he looked at me carefully, making sure I was alright. He then calmly smiled and turned over. "Good night, mommy!" I looked over at Kyla and saw that she was still talking with Dwight. Fortunately, she didn't hear our conversation. I quickly left the room and walked back to my room.

I flung myself to my knees on the carpet and cried "My son, my son." Then I surrendered him back to the Lord. "Whatever brings You greater glory Lord. Please help me have Your kingdom perspective. Remind me that we're just passing through and that no matter what, I'll live eternity in heaven with Kairos and with Koby (our 1st son who's already there)."

3/8/10
Journal Entry:

I saw a picture of Kairos. He was with Jesus. Jesus had already turned and was walking away. Kairos was holding His hand but before he turned to follow, he said with a huge smile, "Bye Mommy!" In the distance, I saw a hill with 3 crosses on it. I bawled and wept. "Lord!" I cried, "it's so hard!" Then I surrendered my son back to Jesus.

––––––

I honestly don't know specifically what is going to happen to my son Kairos but Dwight and I both sense that the Lord may ask this of our son—to lay down his life for His King. Apart from the strength of His Spirit, it is impossible for me to willingly surrender him to Jesus when I think about my precious son and the possibility of him suffering/dying. But over and over again, Jesus keeps asking me to surrender Kairos back to Himself. I believe it is the goodness of our Lord that He is doing this to prepare us for what is ahead, whatever that may look like or be.

As we approach our Lord's coming, all of us are being asked to lay down our lives for our King. And to be honest, if you are reading this book and have gotten this far, you are willing to do so. But I believe that perhaps the more difficult thing is being asked from those of us who are parents or grandparents. Our two generations are being asked something even harder to give up than our own lives. We're being asked to surrender our children/grandchildren to the destiny and calling on their lives, which may include dying for our King. I know that part of the purpose of writing this book is to do just that—to prepare our hearts to give up our greatest treasure on Earth—our children & grandchildren and to lay them at His feet. It is vital for us to have His kingdom perspective if we are to walk victoriously through the coming days and years when darkness will cover the Earth like never before. If not, we may become embittered against our King, our love may grow cold and we may walk away because we think it's too costly or too difficult to follow Him.

I love the following chorus from an old hymn:

"Jesus paid it all, ALL to Him I owe, sin hath left a crimson stain, He washed it white as snow."

𝔥e is worth it all.

4/26/06-
Journal Entry:
2:26 am

As I thought about Kairos, and the calling on his life, my heart aches and then another poem is born.

"Surrender . . . again"

His smile melts my heart as his happy eyes fill my soul with joy
His laughter is contagious as his head flings backwards
His eyes squint and his mouth opens wide as hearty sounds
of deep laughter fill the room
Chasing away the sadness, despair and gloom.

He runs over to me and looks deep into my eyes.
"I wuv you Mommy" he gently whispers as he wraps his little
arms around my neck.
I melt as he pours love all over me.

How can a 4 year old contain such supernatural joy and
love?

Only by the grace of a supernatural God.

"Mommy" he proclaims.
"My God wuvs me, and I wuv my God!" with a huge smug
smile on his precious lil' face.

"Mommy, me sad. Jesus died on cross. I sad. BUT mommy,
Jesus alive! I happy."

How can a 4 year old grasp the crucifixion and resurrection?
Only by the merciful hand of a supernatural sovereign LORD.

"Mommy, I die for God. No, not did, not do. Mommy, I die
for God. Mommy, it's okay, I here for awhile."

How can a 4 year old know his destiny?
Only by the supernatural revelation given to him by a
supernatural powerful God.

How can I possibly surrender my precious son to God?
Only by the supernatural power, grace, courage, faith and
strength that only my God Jesus can give.

To live is Christ. To die is gain.

Lord, I surrender my son to you . . . again.
My emotions and feelings cry out "NO! Not yet!!
It's too hard!!"
Yet . . .
I know and feel Your pleasure in my surrender . . . in my
sacrifice.

Who am I that I should withhold anything from You?

You are the Giver of all good gifts.
You gave me my children and appointed me steward/
guardian
Over them. But they belong to You.

Whatever brings You greater glory LORD.
My son is Yours, not mine.
I surrender.

Chapter 16
We are keys to the kingdom of heaven.
It is time to ARISE & SHINE!

12/30/09
Journal Entry:
2:22 am

As I sat at a computer in our home looking for an article I wrote earlier to finish this book, the clock caught my eye. 2:22 My heart smiled. Jesus had been putting this number in front of me all week long to remind me of my life verse that He had given to me a few years ago.

Isaiah 22:22 (ESV)
"And I will place on his shoulder the key of the house of David.
He shall open, and none shall shut; and he shall shut, and none shall open."

I raised my hands in the air as my heart responded to His love. Suddenly, my hands got super heavy. My initial response was to assume it was because it was filled with keys. That's what He's done before. As my hands kept dropping from the weight I felt on them, I looked at my open palms expecting to see keys. I was surprised when I saw instead that my palms were colored with a metallic color. I asked Jesus what this meant. And He began to speak. "Liza, you don't just hold keys to My kingdom. You **are** a key to the kingdom of heaven. So is Dwight and every single child of Mine." I was puzzled. "Jesus, I believe You when You say I am a key. But how does this work?" Immediately I got the following picture. I could see myself talking to a lost soul. As I spoke life to this person, I could see my words becoming like tiny little keys that would unlock layers around this person's heart so that they became more open to Jesus. I watched as another person did an act of kindness like helping the poor. And I watched as this act of kindness touched the unsaved person's heart, and layers that covered this person's heart, like layers of an onion, began to be removed.

Then the Lord continued. "Liza, every city has gates to them. And some individuals are chosen to be a key to their city." At this point, He reminded me of this past Sunday, when Pastor Cal Chinen's wife, Joy, had prayed over Dwight and me. In the spirit, she was given a key and then the Lord told her that she was a key. Then she prayed for us, that like her, we would be keys to our city as well. I thought to myself "Cool!! But how does that work? How are we keys to our city?" Then Jesus reminded me of a cartoon that I had just watched, Monsters vs. Aliens. "Remember that part where the man put his hand on that computerized screen? It was his fingerprints and eye pattern, etc. that was the key to opening that authorized doorway. You need to think of keys in a new way to understand how you are literally a key to My kingdom. It's not just about holding a piece of metal and sticking it into a keyhole in the door."

Then He brought to my mind a picture of one of the main gatekeepers for my city of Hilo. I watched as she put her hand onto a panel that checked her handprint. And once she was cleared, the authorized door opened.

Then the Lord said, "Liza, every family also has a doorway over them." Then I watched as I saw fathers and husbands taking their rightful place of authority over their families. And as they did that, they became the keys to opening heaven over their families and marriages.

Jesus continued. "Do you see that being a key on Earth is tied in with spiritual authority? When you walk in true spiritual authority that I have given and NOT man, you become that key of My kingdom on Earth. Be the key you were destined to be!"

I could tell the Lord was quite indignant about those on Earth that were self-appointed leaders. "Liza, these do NOT carry My authority. Even demons recognize this. Remember those 7 sons of Sceva? They wanted the power and recognition. But they carried no true spiritual authority. In these last days, all those in My last days army will walk in true spiritual authority. Know who you are. Know and understand your identity in Me through the cross and the power of My blood that covers all your sins. Be the key I destined you to be! Walk into your destiny. This is My Kingdom Perspective."

——————

There's a song that I heard while I was working on the rough draft of this manuscript. It is entitled "Through Heaven's Eyes" from the movie—*The Prince of Egypt* (UNI/DreamWorks, 1998, music and lyrics by Stephen Schwartz; vocals by Brian Stokes Mitchell). As I watched this beautiful moving film with my children and as I heard this particular song, I began to weep as I realized how powerfully it captured the heart of what it meant to see one's worth and self through God's heavenly perspective.

This song was filled with thought provoking questions. If I imagined that I was a single thread in a tapestry, could I really see my value and worth if I just looked at myself as that single thread? Or did I need to see the whole tapestry to then realize how my piece fitted into the bigger picture and then to see my worth from that perspective? If I imagined that I was the large stone positioned at the peak of a mountain top, was I more important than the stones that was located at the mountain's base? If I was a sheep lost in the forest, wasn't my shepherd worth more to me than the richest King in the land? If I was dying of thirst in a desert, wasn't a cool fresh spring worth more to me than a lake of gold?

As the song continued, it asked several significant questions: How do we determine what our lives are truly worth? How do we measure the value of a person? Do we measure by size, strength, and wealth? Do we measure a person by how much he/she has gained in this world or by how much they gave? What if a person lost everything? Is this person now worthless? Then the song made a revelatory statement: "You can never see with your eyes on earth." As the song closed, it powerfully concluded that the true answer to these questions came when we looked at our lives through heaven's eyes: through the loving eyes of our Father In heaven and through the loving eyes of our Lord Jesus.

Dear brothers and sisters in Christ, we need to see our worth and value on Earth through God's perspective, not our own fleshly ones. You and I need to know who we are in the deepest parts of our hearts. We are sons and daughters of the King of Kings. We need to know and understand our identity in Christ through the cross and because of the power of His blood that covers **all** our sins. When we truly see ourselves the way God sees us, You and I will be the keys He destined us to be! See & believe. Then rise up and walk into your destiny. This is His Kingdom Perspective.

*Kingdom Perspective:
ARISE & SHINE!

Isaiah 60:1-3(ESV)
"Arise, shine, for your light has come, and the glory of the LORD has risen upon you. For behold, darkness shall cover the earth, and thick darkness the peoples; but the LORD will arise upon you, and his glory will be seen upon you. And nations shall come to your light, and kings to the brightness of your rising."

As I end this book, I want to share this final Kingdom Perspective. It is actually a call that He is sending out in this hour. Family of God, it is time to arise and shine. As I read Isaiah 60:1-3, I really like verse one. "Arise, shine, for your light has come, and the glory of the LORD has risen upon you." This is encouraging and life giving. Verse two, however, I'd rather skip. "For behold darkness shall cover the earth and thick darkness the peoples." But it is truth and we need to see the whole truth and the bigger picture so that we can be prepared for what is already happening—the darkness that is covering the earth and the peoples of the earth.

There will be increasing suffering and darkness such as we've never seen before as the end approaches. We can already see this happening. And yet, the hope and truth is that as the darkness increases in the world, so is the light that will increase in us. We are the light of world. A city on a hill can't be hidden. If we don't arise and shine, the world will remain in darkness. Come on Church. It is time to wake up! It is time to see things as He sees things and to see ourselves as He sees us. It is vital that we arise and shine His glory, and be the loving, humble hands and feet of Jesus to a lost and dying world.

2/25/08
Journal Entry:

During my soaking/prayer time with Jesus, I sensed Him asking me to sing to Him. So I did. Then I could see a huge open field with flowers in it. I saw myself walking through it. Then I saw Jesus. He had me sing a new song. "Arise, shine for My light is upon you. Arise, shine for My glory is in you." It was a beautiful new song. Then Jesus began to sing this new song over me. Then He spoke.

"It is time to arise and shine. Those that are truly seeking and hungering for Me will arise and they will shine. There will be no more playing games in the church. Those that truly seek Me will be known by My light and glory shining through them. Those that aren't will **not** carry My authority and anointing. Every one will know and recognize those that truly carry Me."

01/01/10
Journal Entry:

As I waited on the Lord on January 1st, I got the following picture:

I saw Jesus' hand extended out to mine. I grabbed it with joy. Then He took me to a cliff with a huge valley below. It was filled with a huge multitude. Wow! It was His Last Days Army! All of a sudden, I was on the valley floor with Jesus, walking around the army camp. Suddenly, I saw Jesus also on the top of the cliff, yet He was still with me. I looked at Him perplexed. He laughed and said, "Liza, they can't see Me down here. Don't worry, I'm God. I can be in all places at the same time."

When Jesus appeared at the top of the cliff, He appeared as the LORD of HOSTS, a mighty king leading his army. All eyes were glued onto Him.

Then Jesus grew, grew and grew in size. It was amazing to watch. I gasped at His sheer size. I asked Him why He was growing so big. He said it was to remind and show His army how big and powerful He really was.

Suddenly, I found myself back on the cliff looking down at His army with Him. I was really, really small in size next to Jesus. I watched Him passionately looking down at this multitude and then I saw Him hold His hand out towards them. Quietly but calmly, He explained that these were the ones who chose to stand; who crossed the dividing line and chose Him. I felt His pleasure as He continued to gaze upon them.

Then, with His outstretched hand, He yelled and declared, **"RISE UP! RISE UP! RISE UP!"** Each time He said this, I was hit by the power of God. As He spoke, He was releasing something upon His army. And as I watched His army, I saw that they grew in strength.

All of a sudden, I saw a group of people lined up along the ridge of the cliff overlooking the army in the valley. I asked Jesus who they were. He said that these were the ones He's raised up to be spiritual parents to this army. Then it was like I was seeing things from the perspective of one of these spiritual parents. I was standing on a ridge overlooking a small army in a valley, overseeing this group from above.

I asked the Lord, "How are we suppose to do this? (To help watch over and take care of these warriors that were entrusted to us?" Then He reminded me of Moses, Joshua and the battle at Rephidim. Exodus 17:8-13 (NLT)

"While the people of Israel were still at Rephidim, the warriors of Amalek attacked them. Moses commanded Joshua, "Choose some men to go out and fight the army of Amalek for us. Tomorrow, I will stand at the top of the hill, holding the staff of God in my hand." So Joshua did what Moses had commanded and fought the army of Amalek. Meanwhile, Moses, Aaron, and Hur climbed to the top of a nearby hill. As long as Moses held up the staff in his hand, the Israelites had the advantage. But whenever he dropped his hand, the Amalekites gained the advantage. Moses' arms soon became so tired he could no longer hold them up. So Aaron and Hur found a stone for him to sit on. Then they stood on each side of Moses, holding up his hands. So his hands held steady until sunset. As a result, Joshua overwhelmed the army of Amalek in battle.

Although Moses wasn't directly involved in the physical battle as Joshua and His men were, the entire battle's victory was weighted on Moses and on his staff being held up by his hands. He did have helpers who helped keep his hands up in the air. What I personally got from this was that these spiritual parents, although they may not be seen up in the front of battle, they were very important in determining the battle's victory and in helping those they oversaw and mentored.

7/13/10
Journal Entry:

Had a soaking time with my children, waiting together on the Lord—being still and listening. I got the following picture. I saw a battlefield. Yet in the midst of it, our family was having a wonderful picnic with Jesus. It was peaceful, delightful, grassy and beautiful in our picnic spot. Beyond our picnic area was a battlefield. I was reminded that even though we are in the battle, when we are with Jesus, there is peace. Romans 16:20 (NASB) came to mind: "The God of peace will soon crush Satan under your feet." Thanks Lord for Your supernatural peace!

5/30/11
Journal Entry:

I heard Jesus speak the following to my heart:

Do you see the prisoners in the valley? I desire them to be set free. Some of them don't even know they are in prison. There is much work to be done. The prisoners need to be set free first for they are future laborers in the great harvest. In My presence, everything is exposed because of the light. You are the light because you carry My presence inside of you. As you go, people, my prisoners, will begin to see their true condition.

9/10/11
Journal Entry:
I got the following word:

Deep calls to deep. I AM here. The winds are changing. I AM . . . I AM coming. Do you hear the drum beat? I am calling My soldiers. Do you hear Me? It is time to lay aside your plans, your ways, your will and to focus simply and only on Me—My Will, My Glory, My Way. Do not fear. Do not be afraid. I AM calling. I AM calling you to arise. The world needs to see My light. The nations are waiting for My mighty ones to rise up. Will you heed My call? Sound the alarm—the Call to Holiness. My judgments are coming and they will be swift. Be forewarned. Self appointed leaders—STOP STEALING MY GLORY! Stop playing games for your selfish gain. Vengeance is mine. I will repay. STOP STEALING the Glory of God! STOP playing games for your selfish gain!

Seal these things this day with Your blood Jesus. Your Kingdom come, Your Will be done on Earth as it already is in Heaven. Amen.

09/07/12
Journal Entry:
As I waited in silence during a monthly intercessory gate gathering in our city, I got the following: "The Warriors are arising!" As I listened, I could hear the beat of drums in the distance. Jesus spoke once more. "We are entering My finest hour. Do you see?"

I heard the sound of horns blowing from shofars and even conch shells; their sounds mixing in with the beating of the drums. What powerful sounds! And I was hit by the power of God as I listened.

As I was prompted to glance into the distance, I saw a large hoof. As I looked up, I saw a gigantic white horse with Jesus sitting on top of it. The horse stayed in one place but it moved its hooves, up and down. Stomp! Stomp! Stomp! The drumbeats were in sync with its mighty steps. Jesus was dressed as the King of Kings on His horse.

As I looked all around Him, I saw warriors rising up to His call. They were coming from every tribe and nation throughout the Earth. Then they stood as an army in a semi-circle around Him and His horse with all eyes focused on their King. No one moved. Jesus was sitting on his horse but He was now facing His army. It was quiet but intensely calm. All of a sudden, He raised his right hand up towards the sky. In it, He wielded His mighty sword. Then he roared, "Charge!"

The warriors instantly responded and moved forward at His leading.

—

Dear fellow warriors, it is time to arise and shine. Our King has sounded the call to all tribes and nations. Do you see? Do you hear? It is time to charge. Our King Jesus is establishing His Kingdom on Earth in its fullness and He desires to establish it fully in you, in me, and in all those who have faithfully kept their eyes and hearts on Him alone. It is time for us to be the pieces and keys He created us to be in His infinite plan.

As I conclude this book, I want to share a verse that the Lord gave me as one of the confirmations for finishing this manuscript.

Habakkuk 2:2 (ESV)-
And the Lord answered me, "Write the vision, make it plain on tablets so he may run who reads it."

It is my prayer that the Lord would use this book to help you run the race that He has set before you. Thank you for reading these reflections from my times with Jesus in the secret place and reading the word of my testimony. Ultimately, my desire is that you would simply hear Him. If the Lord has allowed the things shared in this book to resonate in your spirit, would you please pray the following with me in agreement?

Prayer/Declaration:
Jesus, we desire to have Your Kingdom Perspective. Change us to become just like You. Transform and renew our minds Lord. Grant us Your Kingdom Perspective that the eyes of our hearts would be illuminated and Your Spirit of wisdom and revelation would flow freely through us. Holy Spirit, fill us up to overflowing and produce the fruit of Your Spirit in us. Cover us with Your mantle of humility and with the full armor of God. Give us Your wisdom, patience, perseverance, and love to faithfully steward the keys of Your kingdom that will bring You glory.
Help us to be faithful and true to the very end.
Father, we declare together that Your Kingdom come, Your will be done through this book and through us on Earth as it

already is in heaven. In Your Name Jesus and by the power
of Your blood, we ask and proclaim these things, Amen.

Thank you for journeying with me.
It is an honor to serve in the Lord's army with you.
Grace, peace & blessings,
Liza

The Kobayashi Family-
Dwight and Liza,
Kyla—our oldest daughter with the hat on,
Kairos—our son & middle child,
Kailee—our youngest child sitting on Liza's lap,
(Koby, our first born child and son who is now in heaven with
Jesus.)

About the Author

Liza is a former high school biology teacher who now is a stay-home mom taking care of her 3 children. She is a writer, teacher, worshipper and prophetic intercessor who loves Jesus, adores her husband Dwight and treasures her kids. Liza currently serves as a regional intercessory gate leader with Transformation Hawaii.

She and her husband Dwight also help to pastor a small church called Elevate and co-own Only Worship Him, a small business dedicated to creating inspirational works for the glory of God.

Her heart's desire is to see her city, state and nation transformed by Jesus and to see His Bride throughout the world rise up, pure and spotless, shining His glorious light. Liza and Dwight, along with their 3 children, live in Hilo, Hawaii.

onlyworshiphim@gmail.com